LOTUS BLOOMS AND FOOT-WIDE PADS NEAR BAYOU LAFOURCHE

AFTER A RARE SNOWFALL IN A CYPRESS SWAMP

SQUADRONS OF BLUE GEESE AGAINST A WINTER'S NIGHT SKY

CYPRESS KNEES AND A CARPET OF DUCKWEED

A SOUTHERN BAYOU CLOGGED WITH WATER HYACINTHS

MOONLIGHT ON MARSHLAND NEAR THE GULF OF MEXICO

FOG-SHROUDED MORNING IN THE ATCHAFALAYA SWAMP

*Other Publications:*

WORLD WAR II
THE GREAT CITIES
HOME REPAIR AND IMPROVEMENT
THE WORLD'S WILD PLACES
THE TIME-LIFE LIBRARY OF BOATING
HUMAN BEHAVIOR
THE ART OF SEWING
THE OLD WEST
THE EMERGENCE OF MAN
THE TIME-LIFE ENCYCLOPEDIA OF GARDENING
LIFE LIBRARY OF PHOTOGRAPHY
THIS FABULOUS CENTURY
FOODS OF THE WORLD
TIME-LIFE LIBRARY OF AMERICA
TIME-LIFE LIBRARY OF ART
GREAT AGES OF MAN
LIFE SCIENCE LIBRARY
THE LIFE HISTORY OF THE UNITED STATES
TIME READING PROGRAM
LIFE NATURE LIBRARY
LIFE WORLD LIBRARY
FAMILY LIBRARY:
   *HOW THINGS WORK IN YOUR HOME*
   *THE TIME-LIFE BOOK OF THE FAMILY CAR*
   *THE TIME-LIFE FAMILY LEGAL GUIDE*
   *THE TIME-LIFE BOOK OF FAMILY FINANCE*

# THE BAYOUS

THE AMERICAN WILDERNESS/TIME-LIFE BOOKS/ALEXANDRIA, VIRGINIA

BY PETER S. FEIBLEMAN
AND THE EDITORS OF TIME-LIFE BOOKS

Time-Life Books Inc.
is a wholly owned subsidiary of
TIME INCORPORATED

FOUNDER: Henry R. Luce 1898-1967

Editor-in-Chief: Hedley Donovan
Chairman of the Board: Andrew Heiskell
President: James R. Shepley
Vice Chairman: Roy E. Larsen
Corporate Editor: Ralph Graves

TIME-LIFE BOOKS INC.

MANAGING EDITOR: Jerry Korn
Executive Editor: David Maness
Assistant Managing Editors:
Dale Brown, Martin Mann
Art Director: Sheldon Cotler
Chief of Research: Beatrice T. Dobie
Director of Photography: Melvin L. Scott
Senior Text Editors:
William Frankel, Diana Hirsh
Assistant Art Director: Arnold C. Holeywell

CHAIRMAN: Joan D. Manley
President: John D. McSweeney
Executive Vice President: Carl G. Jaeger
Executive Vice President: David J. Walsh
Vice President and Secretary: Paul R. Stewart
Treasurer and General Manager:
John Steven Maxwell
Business Manager: Peter B. Barnes
Mail Order Sales Director: John L. Canova
Public Relations Director: Nicholas Benton

THE AMERICAN WILDERNESS
SERIES EDITOR: Charles Osborne
Editorial Staff for The Bayous:
Editor: Harvey B. Loomis
Text Editor: Gerry Schremp
Picture Editor: Patricia Hunt
Designer: Charles Mikolaycak
Staff Writers: Sam Halper, Paul Hathaway,
Don Nelson, John von Hartz
Chief Researcher: Martha T. Goolrick
Researchers: Barbara Ensrud, Beatrice Hsia,
Carol Isenberg, Janice Pikey
Design Assistant: Vincent Lewis

Editorial Production
Production Editor: Douglas B. Graham
Assistant: Gennaro C. Esposito
Quality Director: Robert L. Young
Assistant: James J. Cox
Copy Staff: Rosalind Stubenberg (chief),
Barbara Quarmby, Heidi Sanford,
Florence Keith
Picture Department: Dolores A. Littles,
Joan Lynch

*The Author:* Peter S. Feibleman was reared in New Orleans, and drew on boyhood memories as well as more recent explorations in writing this book. He has contributed two books to the TIME-LIFE Foods of the World series, *American Cooking: Creole and Acadian* and *The Cooking of Spain and Portugal.* His novels include *Strangers and Graves, A Place Without Twilight, The Daughters of Necessity* and *The Columbus Tree.* He has also written for the theater, films and television.

*The Cover:* Bald-cypress trees, characteristically festooned with Spanish moss, are mirrored by the still surface of Lake Dauterive, one of a number of lakes along the Atchafalaya River flood plain, in the heart of southern Louisiana's bayou country.

Valuable assistance was given by the following departments and individuals of Time Inc.: Editorial Production, Michael E. Keene; Library, Benjamin Lightman; Picture Collection, Doris O'Neil; Photographic Laboratory, George Karas; TIME-LIFE News Service, Murray J. Gart.

# Contents

# A Meeting Place for Rivers and the Sea

The waters of half a continent churn south through Louisiana in the formidable currents of the Mississippi and its tributary, the Red River (both shown in white). On the way they feed countless smaller waterways, known in this part of the world as bayous. Neighboring states have bayous, but, as this map demonstrates, Louisiana is quintessential bayou country.

In the northern half of the state most of the terrain is dry and hilly (areas with elevations above 150 feet are indicated by deeper green). In Louisiana's delta region, where the Mississippi and its main distributary, the Atchafalaya, meander to the Gulf of Mexico, the land is mostly flat and mostly wet, with many fresh-water swamps and open, sunlit salt marshes. (Both are marked by blue dashes.) Louisiana's Indian and French heritage is richly recorded in the names of towns and waterways.

The bayous themselves are shown on the map as solid blue lines, as are the Atchafalaya, the smaller rivers and man-made channels. Wildlife refuges and public parks and forests are outlined in red, while a line of blue dots traces the Intracoastal Waterway, an inland route for small boats.

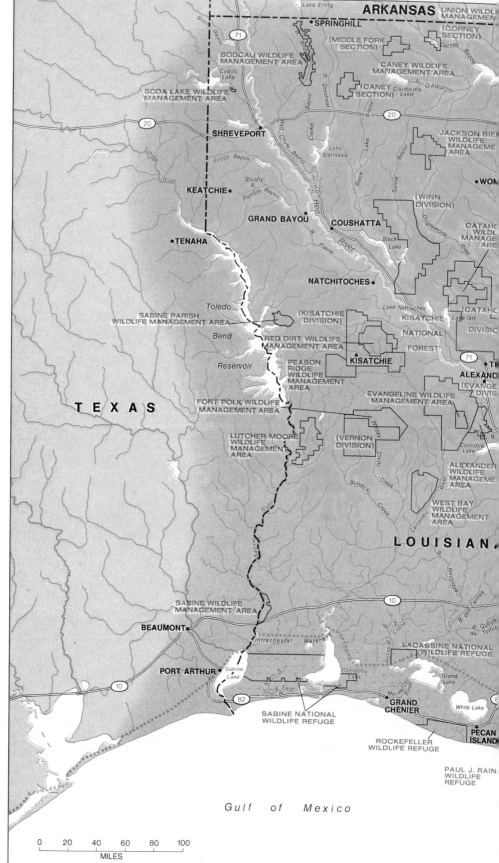

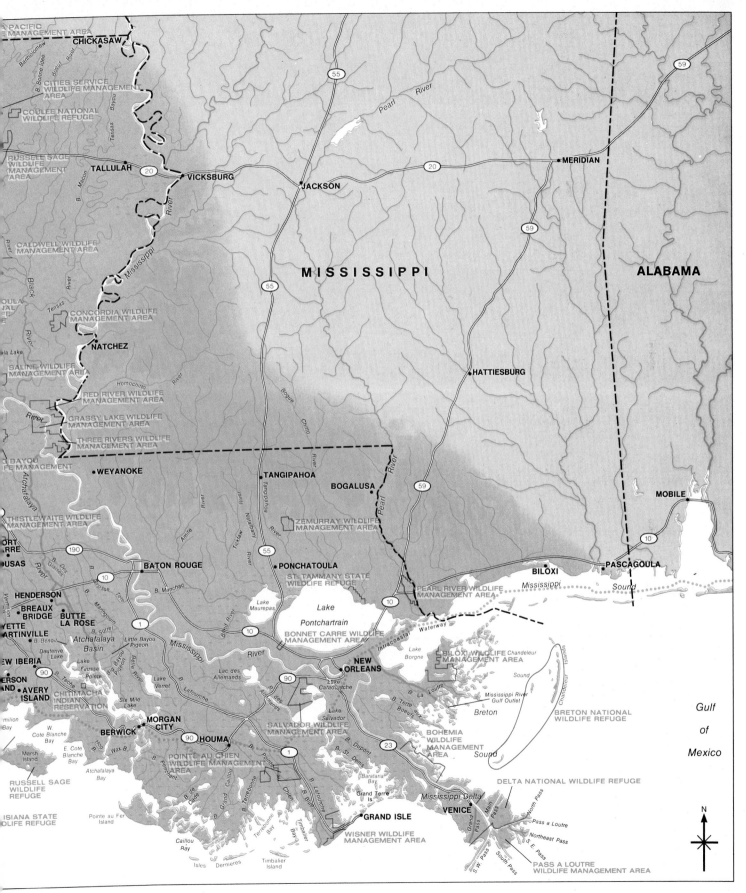

# 1/ The Liquid Land

*It is a place that seems often unable to make up its mind whether it will be earth or water, and so it compromises.* HARNETT T. KANE/ *THE BAYOUS OF LOUISIANA*

Imagine that you are traveling behind a flock of snow geese as they wing south from Canada along the Mississippi Flyway toward the Gulf of Mexico. Follow them into Louisiana and you will recognize the bayou country by its look. Seen from the air, the land appears to be crisscrossed by a lacework of waterways that twist and turn, lashing back and forth. Here and there the lakes, rivers and creeks, the swamps, marshes and smaller patches of dark liquid seem to fill up—to grow solid in some mysterious way—until they turn into vast stretches of dry land rooted with trees, soft with flowers, swathed in grasses.

Move farther south with the wild geese as they look for a place to land; earth that seemed solid appears to melt from under its lush vegetation until it becomes water again. Still farther, the whole country seems to congeal into an amorphous substance whose texture is neither liquid nor solid, but an odd combination of both. Along the Gulf Coast, where the geese will touch down for the winter, streams branch out, disappear, reappear, coincide, mesh, forming a vast patternless pattern that looks, from high above, as though a sheet of dark glass had been shattered in a hundred different directions.

In all, Louisiana has about 3,500 square miles of water surface. Some of that total is accounted for by such enormous lakes as 41-mile-wide Pontchartrain in the east and 15-mile-long Calcasieu in the west, and, most notably, by the lordly Mississippi, which courses from the north of the state to its southernmost tip in a path half a mile wide and 569 miles long. But of the smaller waterways that interlace Louisiana like veins, the most numerous and the most fascinating are the bayous. There are scatterings of bayous in Arkansas, Mississippi and Alabama, but only in Louisiana are they so rife that the state can justly be called bayou country. The term derives from *bayuk*, the Choctaw Indians' word for creek; presumably they passed it on to the early French settlers, who gave it a euphonious lilt. Today geographers use "bayou" to describe a watercourse that serves as a distributary, or natural outlet, of a river. Louisianans prefer to be less precise. Following the Choctaw example, they apply the word to almost every kind of watercourse, whether it is a distributary or a tributary, whether it begins or ends in a river, a lake, a swamp or a marsh.

An exact count of the bayous of Louisiana would be almost impossible. A change in the course of the Mississippi or a flood may cause new bayous to form or old ones to disappear; moreover, many of the smaller ones have never been named. As if to make up for the oversight, those that have been labeled often bear such delightful identities as Bayou Go to Hell, Bayou Funny Louis, and Bayou Mouchoir de l'Ourse (meaning Handkerchief of a She-Bear). But nameless or not, most bayous are simply short creeks. Some, to be sure, are more than 100 miles long and at certain points as wide as a broad river. Yet even these, at other points, become so narrow that mosses hanging in branches on either bank meet in the air above the water.

The bayous are most thickly concentrated in southern Louisiana, in an area roughly the shape of a huge triangle. The apex lies 100 miles north of the Gulf of Mexico, where the formidable Atchafalaya River diverges from the Mississippi. The base is the entire sweep of Louisiana coastline, southeastern corner to southwestern corner, along the Gulf. But every other section of the state—northwestern, northeastern, central—has its bayous as well, in settings that vary markedly according to the terrain and that dispute the Hollywood-fostered image of a prototypical bayou. A bayou may indeed be—as the moviemakers have pictured it—a dark stream closed in by a jungle-like swamp; but it may also look very different.

In the hill country in the northwestern part of the state, for example, a bayou may lie at the base of a 300- or 400-foot eminence—a mountain by Louisiana standards—whose crest is dominated by trees alien to a watery realm. Because in this area the mean water table (the level to which the earth's subsurface is saturated with water) lies 10 to 60 feet below ground, hardwoods like red oak and hickory—which cannot tolerate wet roots—flourish on the heights of the hills. Below the hardwoods are towering pines and dense underbrush, and it is only on the banks of the bayou that water-loving willows and cottonwoods are to be seen. Standing at the top of one of these hills, looking down on its three-storied forest to the bayou far below, a visitor quickly abandons any preconceived notions he may have held about bayous.

He will recapture them, however, as he moves south from the hill country. Gradually the land flattens, turning into a pancake world in which the only significant rises are the natural ridges, called levees, that occur along the banks of rivers and streams. Often the land dips below the water table to become swamp; in this setting, cypress and tupelo-gum trees predominate, and the bayous that thread through the green gloom confirm the romantic image. Along the Gulf Coast, they take on yet another look. In this area of marshland trees thin out; mostly the bayous are fringed with grasses and are wholly open to the sky.

As varied as the settings of the bayous are the movements of their waters. The lively currents of most bayous in the hill country hardly differ from those of larger rivers. But in lower Louisiana the bayous seem to flout hydrological convention; the aura of strangeness that many people sense about a bayou derives in part from this phenomenon.

Early French colonists, who ventured into the swamp wilderness beyond their settlements, wrote back to the mother country about the mysterious bodies of water they had come upon. A bayou, they reported, was "sleeping water," a "dead" stream with no discernible current, altogether a dangerous place for a boatman to find himself. Concerned less with scientific inquiry than with the problems of daily survival, the settlers could not know that "sleeping water" might be the result of a change in the course of the river that originally had fed the bayou. Along the coastal fringes, where fresh and salt water mix, the movements of bayous also appear to defy any rules. Near the Gulf they cannot be said to "run" at all. Instead, they move at their own slow pace in their own manner—and in no definite direction. All day a bayou may flow almost imperceptibly east, emptying into a lake. Then in the evening the bayou will reverse its course and flow westward, draining the same lake. Mysterious as the turnaround seems, it does have a reason: it is a subtle response to changes in the water levels of nearby estuaries that are linked to the flooding and ebbing tides of the Gulf.

To understand the apparent willfulness of the bayou's behavior, it is necessary to know something about the forces that bear upon the land itself. The bayou country is a place where earth and water wage an endless struggle. Its deceptive calm is that of an Eden where time seems to stop; where breezes waft, easy and warm, through great trees and swaying mosses; where streams are gentle; where the humid air appears to magnify the colors of nature; where nearly everything that moves, moves slowly, and where nothing promises to happen—until it happens. Until, that is, the wind rises and this land of slow motion becomes a place of sudden violence. The bayou country is a place of extremes where death mingles with life, in the form of water lurking through the land and over it as well, always posing a lethal threat.

The focal point of the tug of war between land and water is the delta area, where the Mississippi River meets the Gulf of Mexico. By definition a delta is a nearly flat plain through which the diverging branches of a river run as it nears its end. Many people think a delta is carved by a river, as it continuously cuts new channels on its way to the sea. Actually the reverse is true—a delta is built up, not torn down, by a river.

As a river flows on its course, it picks up a burden of sand, silt and clay. The amount of sediment it can carry depends not only on how deep and broad its waters are, but also on how swiftly they move. An enormous river like the Mississippi, running swiftly where the continent is high, carries along with it half a billion tons of sediment a year. At its very end, where the river's fresh water meets the salt water of the Gulf, its velocity is reduced almost to zero and it is forced to drop its silty burden. The waters of the river spread into the sea through distributary channels in a kind of fan shape, like the Greek letter Δ (delta), spreading the sediment in an arc. The currents of the Gulf further distribute the sediment in an even broader sweep. Over the centuries, sediment accumulates to form land masses laced with distributaries that extend the delta farther and farther out into the Gulf.

In the last million years, the location of the Mississippi Delta has changed with the coming and going of each ice age. While the glaciers that covered the continent did not reach as far south as the Gulf of Mexico, Gulf waters—like those of other seas—nourished the glaciers, in the form of water vapor that turned to snow and then to ice. As the great freeze continued, no water returned to replenish the oceans, and the sea level dropped. The reverse occurred when the climate warmed and the glaciers melted: the sea level rose. These rises and falls were no minor matters; each could measure as much as 450 feet, drastically shifting the shorelines. In the last ice age, which ended about 10,000 years ago, the sea level of the Gulf dropped so that the Louisiana coastline extended 50 to 100 miles farther south than where it is now. With the return of warmth and the retreat of the ice, rising Gulf waters flooded northward to a point about 100 miles inland from today's Louisiana coast. By about 3,000 years ago, when the sea level stabilized at its present height, the modern, postglacial Mississippi delta system, starting at what is now the juncture of the Atchafalaya and Mississippi rivers, was already 3,000 years old.

In the process of carrying sediment to its mouth and building up more land, a river gradually lengthens the route it must follow to the sea. Finally it becomes so long that when its upstream banks overflow during flood stage, the rushing waters desert the usual channel and adopt another, shorter route to the sea—a route that then becomes the river's main channel. This has happened to the Mississippi many times during the last 6,000 years or so, and each time the river has shifted, it has created a new subdelta and forsaken an old one. Each time a subdelta has been created, new bayous have been born to help distribute the Mississippi's flow; and after the main channel of the river has moved elsewhere, the bayous have remained as a watery legacy.

Five subdelta regions together now make up what is called the Mississippi Delta, a great triangle nearly 150 miles at its base. The base, however, is anything but straight-edged; the river's restless shiftings, depositing its burden of sediment here, there and everywhere, have produced a series of overlapping, irregular lobes. The subdelta where the Mississippi now flows—Louisianans call it the true delta—has a shape geographers describe as a bird's foot. Curiously, the name has remained apt even though the delta has been extending at the rate of about 200 feet per year. On late-19th Century maps, it resembled an eagle's foot with a narrow shank and four sharp talons. Today it has filled out along the edges and looks more like the webbed foot of a duck.

In the "true" delta, land is encroaching on the Gulf's domain. Along the rim of the subdeltas that the river has abandoned, the Gulf in the main is winning its battle with the land; that part of the southeastern coastline is retreating slowly and steadily into the bayous.

Along the muddy southwestern fringe of Louisiana, the struggle between earth and water has taken a different form, but one in which the Mississippi has also played a role. As the river was building its westernmost subdeltas, some of the sediment it carried washed out to sea and was borne farther west by Gulf currents. During times of storm,

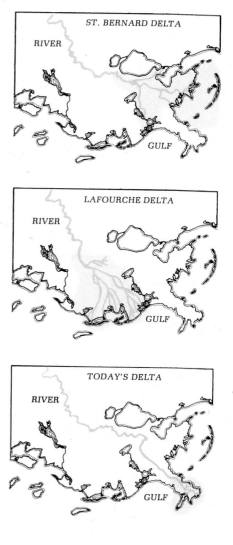

Three of the delta areas that have been formed over the centuries by the Mississippi River as it has shifted its course in flowing to the Gulf of Mexico are shown in blue on the maps above, each superimposed on an outline of modern southern Louisiana. The St. Bernard Delta began building 4,700 years ago, the Lafourche Delta some 3,500 years ago, and today's still-expanding delta about 600 years ago.

waves picked up this sediment and piled it onto the beaches in ridges that paralleled the shore. Varying from a few yards to 30 miles in length, and from 2 to 10 feet in height, these ridges formed barricades of mud, silt and shells where plants could grow, safe from salt water.

The ridges are called cheniers, from the French *chêne*, meaning oak, because they are places where live oaks flourish—and the clinging roots of the trees, in their turn, help to hold the land fast against battering waves. Over the centuries, as Gulf currents have brought more and more river sediment to this western shore, the coastline has crept south, ridge by ridge. A measure of its penetration into the Gulf is that in some places the parallel ranks of cheniers are 10 miles deep. But they are far from invulnerable; high winds and waves can demolish the cheniers altogether, breaking them down and spreading their substance around marshy wetlands that range as far as the eye can see.

The role of water in the bayou country does not end with its shaping of the land. Under the hot sun that beats down on Louisiana most of the year, water continually evaporates, rises, condenses and drops—contributing to rainfall that averages 4.6 inches a month. Again because of water, the high temperatures that prevail except in the brief winters are coupled with high humidity, which hovers at 70 to 80 per cent year round. The idea of high humidity is an abstraction for people who have not lived in this kind of climate; the presence of water vapor in the atmosphere is a tangible, grueling fact, especially during the summer, for those who live here. Extreme humidity reduces evaporation and the effectiveness of the body's cooling system. In similar temperatures on a desert you may be parched—in the bayou country you will be drenched.

Another result of humidity is that clouds writhe and wrinkle and swirl continually overhead as water does on the land below, making the skies among the most beautiful anywhere in the world. Most of the time the clouds are driven by the gentle Gulf winds—breezes, really. But one fact should be kept firmly in mind by any wilderness traveler in the bayou country: the sense of vast peace felt on bayou waters—the serenity that makes it seem as though the earth itself had stopped turning—that serenity can, at a moment's notice, explode into a *Walpurgisnacht* of the skies in which all life is endangered. For evidence there are the great live oaks of the cheniers. Winds have bent, whipped and savaged these trees so often that they have taken on extraordinary convulsed and agonized shapes. Lying at the southern fringe of the bayou country, they are like tree-demons that have been set there to warn the adventurer of what he may expect in the region round about.

Two kinds of winds are to be dreaded: tornadoes and hurricanes. Tornadoes strike the area an average of four times a year, most frequently in spring. A tornado is generally only 400 yards wide, follows a track only a few miles long, and usually travels at about 30 to 40 miles per hour, but it is the most violent kind of storm in nature. A tornado's winds, too furious to measure but estimated to reach a speed of 450 to 500 miles per hour, leave total havoc in their wake.

Even so, hurricanes are more fearsome because of the size of their swath: a hurricane can be 100 miles across, and the high winds and torrential rains around it may extend another 100 miles. From late summer through autumn, a hurricane can rise out of the sea like an aerial monster to overwhelm the land, its winds reaching speeds of 150 to 200 miles per hour. The winds and the rain are accompanied by an invasion of the sea that can flood the low-lying coastal areas with a deluge of salt water more than 15 feet deep. Farther inland, rainfall of up to 10 inches in 24 hours can cause destructive flooding without any help from the sea. Hurricanes strike Louisiana in full force on an average of once every four or five years. But when they hit, everything in their path is in danger of being ripped, torn apart, drowned and buried.

It is a remarkable characteristic of the bayou country, however, that even a killing hurricane can have a beneficial result. Silt stirred up by the storm and redistributed over the marshes by waves may enhance their fertility; more plants will grow to replace those that have died. The vegetation that has managed to survive in and around this country despite periodic natural disasters does so with a kind of wild beauty and an intensity of color; each plant or tree seems to be living at its peak during any given moment of its existence. Both the piny upland bayous and the cypress-filled swamps are dotted with color from early spring to late fall. Bright wild flowers grow like badges of bravura.

Hibiscus, wild iris, spider lilies and pond lilies decorate the freshwater marshes next to sheets and masses of the loveliest bayou flower of all, the water hyacinth—a bloom whose delicate appearance is belied by its habits. For just as a hurricane can be life-giving in this place of extremes, so the elegant hyacinth can be death-dealing.

A solid layer of hyacinths stretching from bank to bank on the surface of a bayou is an extravagant sight, like a river of orchids. Each lavender blossom—pale, with a dab of yellow on the center petal—is surrounded by bright green leaves; its roots dangle invisibly in the water below. The color of the petals shifts faintly with the light, as if reflecting the changing skies, so that the bayou seems to shimmer from lavender to dark purple and back again with the passing of a cloud. And yet the story of the water hyacinth is a story of blossoming death.

It is a flower that might well serve as a prime example of the dangers of tampering with the ecological balance of a wild area. Its story begins in 1884, during the International Cotton Exposition of New Orleans, when exhibits were shipped to the city from a great many foreign countries. Among them, reportedly, was a Japanese exhibit that featured a flowering aquatic plant that was actually native to Latin America. Each visitor to the exhibit received one of the flowers as a souvenir—an attractive bloom that looked like a water orchid. Shortly thereafter, fountains and fish pools and ponds in the city—as well as in the surrounding countryside—were filled with the blossoms.

What people did not know was that this flower was able to reproduce in ways, and on a scale, that are frightening in their ramifications. It did not grow just where it was planted, but soon began to invade the bayous. Birds and storms carried its seeds deep into the swamps, and within a few years a problem of heroic proportions had arisen.

The reproductive system of the water hyacinth is something to marvel at. It is endowed with a means of self-pollination, and can also reproduce by root offshoots. In water that moves as sluggishly as it does in the bayou country, hyacinths can double in number every two weeks. A single plant can produce 65,000 others in a single season. One acre of flowering hyacinths may contain anywhere from 50 to 800 million seeds. Although only 5 per cent usually germinate the next season, many of the rest of the seeds stay dormant. These, however, are still to be reckoned with. They may germinate any time within the next 20 years.

As many as 900,000 plants can float in just one acre of water, and what is so lovely-looking above the surface is not so gentle underneath. A mat of hyacinths eventually may become a floating island in which alligator weeds, cattails, even willow trees can grow, and the stream will be no longer navigable. Below, the vegetation is deprived of light; photosynthesis—the process by which plants use energy from the sun to produce food—is not possible. The plants below the hyacinths die. Phytoplankton disappears and with it the fish. The pond weeds on which ducks feed go—and so, of course, do the ducks.

Along with its ability to reproduce, the hyacinth's indestructibility has over the years become the theme of a sort of black comedy whose setting is the bayou country. As early as 1897, the U.S. Army Corps of Engineers was called in to destroy the plants. Then other federal agencies as well as state conservation authorities joined the fight against the delicate flower—and the delicate flower won.

The record of attempts to destroy it—attempts made on and off over the course of four decades—reads like a script written by Charlie Chaplin in collaboration with W. C. Fields. The first weapon used by the Corps of Engineers was the pitchfork. The choice was somewhat naïve. A great many of the plants were forked onto the banks of bayous; but while they were being thrown up to rot and die, others were reproducing faster than ever as the water was cleared.

In 1900, a sternwheeler was brought, at some expense and difficulty, into the bayous. It had a four-foot conveyor-belt attachment that picked up the hyacinths, chewed them into pulp, and spit them back out. The result was disappointing, and history shows that the men who were trying to get rid of the flower understandably lost their tempers—they soon turned to dynamite. The wilderness boomed with explosion after explosion. Everything in the immediate vicinity of each explosion was destroyed—everything but the hyacinths, thanks to the redoubtable ability of their seeds to sprout after long dormancy. A bayou can be completely cleared on the surface, and can stay clear for a number of years; then the seeds germinate and the hyacinths rise again—and very soon after that the bayou is once more covered by a mass of flowers.

After dynamite proved useless, a flame thrower was paddled up into the bayous. The *Louisiana Conservationist,* published by the state's Wild Life and Fisheries Commission, carried an account: "A full cone of fire, hot enough to melt a block of steel, was squirted on a hyacinth raft. When the fuel was exhausted, a frog emerged from the blackened mat and began sunning itself. The scientist using the flame thrower was even more astounded later during the next growing season. The burnt plants were not only the first to sprout but also averaged nine inches taller than surrounding plants."

After fire, arsenic was tried. Some of its loose powder got into the food of the workers at the site, resulting in the death of one man and the critical illness of 13 others. The hyacinths grew on. Finally, in the 1940s, the Corps employed a weapon that would kill the plants if not the seeds, and that would not harm men or the fish, fowl or animals that used the streams: a chemical called 2,4-D.

So now hyacinths can be kept under control to a certain extent—with vigilance and the expenditure of substantial sums—but they remain fixed inhabitants of the bayou country. They have outlasted not only

*Flashing his white rump patch in alarm, a young buck hightails it through a fresh-water marsh near the Mississippi River, heading for a thicket and safety. The deer of Louisiana's marshes, a subspecies of the common white-tailed deer, have slightly larger hoofs for extra support in the spongy terrain.*

several generations of men intent upon killing them, but also natural calamities like hurricanes, which may wipe out other plants but only spread hyacinths. Wherever you go in the bayous, at a turn in a stream or behind a clump of cypress, you can see a fragile lavender blossom whose petals tremble in the slightest breeze: the survival flower.

The creatures of the bayous are as profuse as the plants. Flying squirrels and gray squirrels thrive in the wooded northern bayous; chipping sparrows and red-cockaded woodpeckers nest in the pine trees, and the streams hold largemouth bass, bream and white crappie (known locally as sac-a-lait) as well as bullfrogs, harmless water snakes and less harmless copperheads, cottonmouths and eastern coral snakes. In the swampy jungle bayous farther south, white-tailed deer run, mourning doves coo, barred owls hoot from the branches overhead, and cicadas shrill underfoot. Providing a counterpoint to these sounds are the noisy munchings of gatherings of huge lubber grasshoppers, three-inch-long creatures that have presumably derived their descriptive name from the popular local term for a clumsy fellow. In the backwaters, countless little prehistoric-looking crawfish breed, along with musk turtles and snapping turtles and several species of salamander.

Farther south, in the marshes, fur-bearing animals like muskrat and nutria abound, sharing the waters with crabs, shrimp, oysters and alligators. Here the skies often teem with birds; the Louisiana coastal region is North America's greatest winter resort for migratory ducks and geese. It is also the spring breeding ground for such wading birds as the snowy and great egrets, and the year-round home of the brown pelican.

In a land where water and land themselves are forever switching places, change of any sort should come as no surprise. The changes hardest to adjust to are those that men have wrought. I have compared parts of the bayou country today with my childhood memories. Bayou Teche, for instance, in the south-central part of the state, is still beautiful. It is perhaps Louisiana's most celebrated bayou, along whose banks grand and elegant houses have stood for well over a hundred years. Nowhere else are there so many live oaks; in no other bayous do the trees grow to such size. Some have trunks nearly 20 feet in girth, wildly twisted giants whose branches stretch out into vast moss-draped tents, mingling their leaves with other trees, standing guard over the water. But the little towns I remembered along the Teche have grown into big ones over the past few decades, and there are only occasional stretches today where the banks are untamed and uninhabited.

The differences in the great swampland known as the Atchafalaya

River Basin are more vivid. The building of flood-control locks at the river's juncture with the Mississippi, and the deepening of the Atchafalaya's main channel to prevent it from overflowing, have diverted much of the water the swamp needs to maintain its level. The expansion of farming and industry, in the drained areas especially, has brought new dams, dikes and highways. As man has advanced, the swamp has retreated, leaving a trail of cypresses standing like gaunt skeletons in the parched earth. Even the sweet gum and palmetto are endangered as their seedlings are attacked by rabbits or rooted up by armadillos that are found in ever-increasing numbers as more land is drained. Fishing holes have dried up, but the white-tailed deer are flourishing, using shrubs and saplings for forage. Though the cougar and the red wolf are nearly gone, the black bear has been saved from extinction by the importation of cubs from Minnesota.

Fortunately, not all of the bayou country has been civilized yet. In the south-central part of the Atchafalaya Basin there are still places where the only movement to be seen is that of an alligator gliding through the water, or a heron swooping down on a crawfish.

Bayou Dorcheat in northern Louisiana was seriously polluted by oil-field salt and gravel washings in the 1940s and 1950s, but these problems have been largely solved; even the gravel strip-mining that persists along parts of its outer fringes has not spoiled the stream itself. And to the angler's added delight, Lake Bistineau—into which the Dorcheat empties—has been dammed, turning it from a swamp into an enormous clear-water lake. At the opposite end of the bayou country, along the coast, oil fields have indeed altered the skyline with their drilling gear, and allowed salt water to spill into fresh-water areas through man-made canals. Even so, much of the marshland remains untouched and as inaccessible as ever, and broad bands of it—totaling some 600,000 acres—are wildlife refuges.

However much they may change, the bayous remain a touchstone for anyone who comes to know them. "When you visit here, you never truly leave," they say in southern Louisiana. Something about these places becomes a part of your life and gives it added meaning. That is the truth that makes a journey into the bayou country worthwhile.

# A Rivalry of Earth and Water

In southern Louisiana the bayou country is a place of innumerable subtle variations on the theme of earth versus water. Most of the land is flat, and all of it is wet or moist; what is solid and what is not is often difficult to discern.

Two rivers—the Mississippi and its major distributary, the Atchafalaya—have been chiefly responsible for shaping and defining the lower bayou country. Flowing southward toward their rendezvous with the Gulf of Mexico, they meander slowly through level land, constantly building and taking away, in the process altering both the landscape and their own channels; in the case of the Mississippi, its changes in course cause variations in its length of as much as 50 miles a year.

Both rivers roll past woods and fertile fields, swamps and marshes, here and there spreading out to linger in shallow basins choked with lush vegetation. As they go, they nourish countless bayous: streams, creeks, ponds that make the countryside a watery patchwork. At spring floodtime, when the current's measured pace becomes a roaring rampage, huge areas are inundated with the rivers' sediment-laden waters.

Eventually the Mississippi, having traveled approximately 3,800 miles from its beginning, and the Atchafalaya, having traveled some 150, encounter the Gulf. The currents and waves of this sea—the fifth largest in the world—nudge and batter the coastal fringe, and its salt water surges inland on each high tide. Here the resilient land performs the role of a buffer between river and sea, an accommodator of opposing forces. Here, too, fresh and salt waters mix in tidal estuaries and ponds, producing miles of brackish marshes that serve several functions: as a vast nursery for aquatic animals, as a home for numberless amphibians, and as a temporary residence for millions of waterfowl and wading birds. Finally, at the continent's edge, the Gulf takes over but continues the work of shaping the land—extending the coast in some places, eating it away in others.

Because the bayou terrain is so flat, a view from the air is the best way to gain a perspective on the southward progression from river to sea, from fresh to salt water. Cruising the area in a small plane, photographer Russell Munson took the pictures on the following pages—a record of a land where earth and water become almost one.

*Muddy and flooded, the Atchafalaya River snakes southward, soaking the wooded areas on both sides of it. The river, which channels almost a third of the Mississippi's water to the Gulf, also shares the Mississippi's burden of sediment, depositing it liberally along the way and changing the look of the land: the long, crescent-shaped island at right is slowly being built up by river clay, silt and sand.*

The Mississippi courses swiftly past the sheer face of a bank it has bitten into during a previous period of flooding. The bare soil, laced with a tangle of exposed tree roots, is evidence that the river has undercut the bank and sliced off a chunk, trees and all. New vegetation may grow to cover the denuded earth—until the next time the waters rise to attack it.

The three dry ridges rising from the flooded lowlands are natural levees built by the Mississippi. Such low ridges are formed during successive flood periods when the water overflows its banks and, with room to spread, slows suddenly and drops much of its sediment. Some natural levees have been added to by men; these remain as the river shaped them.

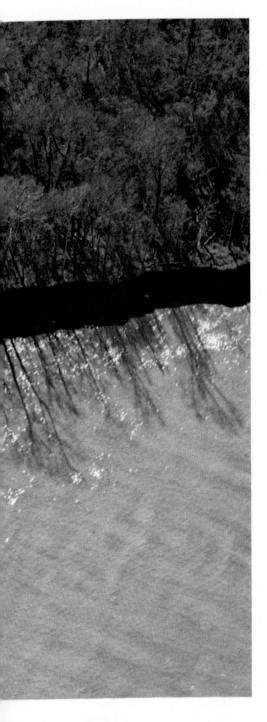

Countless thousands of pale green
water-hyacinth plants blanket a pond
in the 1,900-square-mile Atchafalaya
Basin and inexorably invade a mixed
stand of cypress, tupelo-gum and
willow trees. Beautiful but pestilential,
the water hyacinth grows nearly
everywhere in the fresh-water bayous,
clogging the waterways, choking
out other vegetation and cutting off
the sunlight necessary for aquatic life.

A few miles inland from the Gulf of Mexico, this marshy pond—a so-called mixing bowl—is one of thousands in southern Louisiana in which fresh and salt water blend, producing the brackish broth that fosters rich aquatic life. Fresh water enters the pond from small bayous (top and sides). At high tide, salty water enters through the sinuous tidal inlet (bottom), and the waters mix; at low tide, the blend flows out toward the Gulf.

The salt water of the Gulf, coffee colored by river sediment, washes a marsh at the brink of the southern bayou country. The briny bath nourishes a variety of vegetation. Oyster grass grows on the raised ridge at the water's edge; right behind is wire grass, a salt-tolerant marsh plant that threatens to overrun the dark patches of three-cornered grass (top left), which is favored by the muskrats and nutria that inhabit the marsh.

Tidal ponds, inlets and estuaries
spangle a trackless coastal marsh in
southeastern Louisiana. Their calm,
protected waters, warm and brackish,
constitute one of the world's finest
aquatic nurseries. They also provide an
abundant larder for the many
creatures, such as shrimp, sea trout and
channel bass, that grow to maturity
here before entering the Gulf to spawn.

A ridge of solid earth, called a chenier,
rises from a wet coastal marsh,
providing a foothold for live-oak trees
in an otherwise watery habitat. Such
ridges, named after the French
word for oak, chêne, may extend as far as
30 miles. They were once beaches
marking the edge of the Gulf, formed
by wave action that deposited a
mixture of river sediments and broken
shells from the Gulf's own bottom.

Sea water swirling over the Chandeleur Islands, about 20 miles off the Louisiana coast, testifies to the Gulf's triumph over land that once belonged to the bayou country. These islands were once part of the old St. Bernard Delta when it marked the mouth of the Mississippi (page 24). After the river shifted course, much of the old delta was gradually submerged in the Gulf's waters, leaving a few islands, such as the Chandeleurs, to be buffeted by the Gulf's restless waves and currents.

# 2/ A Difference of Bayous

*And there are the bayous — the Boeuf and the Teche,
Bayou LaFourche, and some whose names are known only
to the moss pickers and the fishermen.*

CHARLES EAST/ *THE FACE OF LOUISIANA*

There are no mountains around southern Louisiana, not even any real hills, and as a child growing up in New Orleans I had never seen the earth look anything but flat. So, one summer when Richard Breaux's father offered to take me with them for a week-long canoe trip on Bayou Dorcheat I was as unprepared for the rolling countryside of northern Louisiana as I was for the wilderness we found there. I was 10 years old at the time and, though I didn't realize it, I was about to discover the northern bayou country in the best manner possible, under the tutelage of a man who had spent a good deal of his life studying and appreciating the face of nature in Louisiana.

Springhill, the nearest town to what would be our starting point for the journey down Bayou Dorcheat, is in the northwest corner of the state; and since New Orleans lies in the southeast, it was a long way from one place to the other. I couldn't for the life of me understand why anybody would want to drive the better part of a day just to go canoeing on a bayou. On the edge of a park not far from where I lived there was a small natural canal that I knew as Bayou St. John; I had often played on its banks. All the other streams I had seen on family picnics looked more or less like Bayou St. John, only not as well manicured. So, for most of the early hours of the drive I dozed, dreaming of other, greater adventures.

At that point I had never even heard of Bayou Dorcheat, but it is a long stream and once it was a famous one. It follows a southerly course for 122 miles from Nevada County, Arkansas, through northern Louisiana to Lake Bistineau, where it empties. The lake feeds into Loggy Bayou, which then drains into the Red River, which in turn leads to the Mississippi. Until about the time of the Civil War, the Dorcheat was an important north-south waterway with sawmills and gristmills, wharves and warehouses along its banks. The virgin pine forests provided choice timber and, after they had been cut, farmers settled in. In 1873, the Red River was cleared of accumulated log jams and steamboat traffic left the Dorcheat for the Red's larger channel. As lumber companies moved away and farmers abandoned their weevil-plagued lands, the Dorcheat gradually reverted to its natural state, becoming a kind of second-generation wilderness.

As we headed toward it that day in the early 1940s, I woke from my dreams with a sense of alarm. The road was dipping up and down as if it had hiccups, and outside the car windows the earth rolled and curled in every direction. I was seeing my first hills. We had made a detour into the Kisatchie National Forest, where we could find a picnic table and an outdoor grill for roasting hot dogs.

To me the word "forest" seemed a strange name for the five- to six-foot-tall trees standing beside the road. Richard's father explained that this area had been heavily lumbered until recent years, but that with the Depression the federal government had bought up the land cheaply and was now in the process of replanting the denuded acres with loblolly, slash and longleaf pines. Because the land was assembled piecemeal, the Kisatchie consisted of six separate sections; we were in the northeast one, in the area known as the Catahoula Ranger District.

In the years since then, the sapling pines have grown into towering giants as much as 100 feet high and today's Kisatchie is densely forested, rich in game animals and birds. Even back then, we could see signs of returning wildlife. Close to where we stopped for lunch, I spotted a quail looking for seeds in a patch of burr-spangled beggar's-ticks, oblivious to our intrusion. Later Richard and I went climbing in a grove of sweet gums and red oaks; the lumber companies, interested primarily in pines, had left these hardwoods alone.

Back in the car, we headed northwest again, and as we approached the end of our drive, something about the trees along the road struck me as odd. Directly beneath the tall pines, a band of young broad-leaved trees pushed up from the soil. These were deciduous hardwoods —a mix mostly of white oaks and hickories, sweet gums and elms. A bit farther on, the hardwoods were almost as tall as the pines. Soon there was another change. The deciduous trees had taken over; the pines were nearly all gone. It was as if the first forest had been replaced by the second through some slow-motion sleight of hand.

What I was seeing was three of the stages in the development of a "climax forest"—and what to me appeared as a fairly rapid transformation actually takes several hundred years to accomplish. Whenever tamed land reverts to wilderness, as it had done here, with a new forest rising where an old one has stood, it does so in a series of steps. The successive species of trees vary from region to region, but the firstcomers are always softwoods; and the ultimate survivors, the trees of the climax forest, are always hardwoods.

In the hills along the Dorcheat, the pioneer softwood species is the prolific loblolly pine, augmented by the shortleaf pine. A single loblolly can produce 500 cones a year; each cone holds 70 or 80 seeds. After the cones open, the infinitesimally lightweight seeds are sown widely by winds, and they are able to germinate readily in almost any sunny soil, even soil that is not particularly rich. Within five years or so, the pines can turn a barren acre into a nursery crowded with as many as 5,000 five-foot-high saplings.

After the pines are established, squirrels and birds bring in acorns, nuts and seeds from neighboring hardwood trees. Hardwoods, which can tolerate shade when young, spring up quickly. Pine seedlings, on the other hand, die out if deprived of full sunlight. Over the years, as hardwoods increase in size and number, they appropriate every clearing until they crowd out the pines or kill them with shade. Occasionally a brush fire may give the pines a reprieve by destroying the understory of hardwoods while hardly damaging the pines, which are insulated by thick bark. But hardwoods are longer lived than pines, as well as better equipped to compete for sunlight; and eventually they triumph.

The northern part of Bayou Dorcheat lies in a valley of such hardwoods. Approaching the bayou, we turned off the highway onto a long series of dirt roads that led into open country. We stopped at the top of a steep slope. Below and in front of us the forested hill country of northern Louisiana lay in undulating waves of trees. Under a slate-blue sky the hills stretched away in long and secret splendor. The foreground of bright green gave way to a paler green, then in the distance to a blue-green. Above the trees was a film of glittering dust that suffused the atmosphere with a reddish glow like visible heat. I could not imagine where the red was coming from until I looked down at the earth.

Soil that contains iron oxide is rust colored; the hard topsoil on which we were standing had a baked look, like the surface of a vast irregular brick. I gouged at it with a stick. Underneath, it was even more reddish. The look of the freshly dug soil, turned out over the ground—red on red —became, for me, the look of the Dorcheat. In the silent heat of early summer, a male cardinal flitted out of a branch overhead, brilliant in his crimson feathers—the square root of red, as if he had come from someplace deep in the earth where the color began.

A few minutes later we walked over a high roll of earth down to the bank of Bayou Dorcheat. I knew then that the streams I had seen in New Orleans bore about as much resemblance to a bayou running through wooded country as a man-made canal bears to the Mississippi. The Dorcheat was my first glimpse of an untamed bayou, and I have never forgotten it. At the water's edge a few cypresses bent gracefully over the quiet stream, their knobby knees sticking up out of the water, seemingly separated from the trunks two or three feet away. But there was none of the moss one finds in the south. Here the cypress trees were backed closely by a line of bright green pines. Beside the cypresses, a willow hung above the water, stirring in a faint breeze.

For most of its course, Bayou Dorcheat runs through the wooded hill country, and where we stood its banks rose and dipped in easy arcs until the stream curved out of sight. Beyond the cypresses and pines and hardwoods, I could see a solitary patch of bamboo, looking tropical and out of place.

We pitched camp in a small clearing near the water's edge and there, in the light of late afternoon, Richard and I played tag. On the hill that rose several hundred yards from the bayou, purple blossoms of verbena flashed, and a tangle of yellow-petaled black-eyed Susans cascaded down the slope. The hillside drew us, and we climbed it. From a height the bayou looked like a stream of molten lead cooling as the day waned. It flowed faster than the bayous I came to know in later years, but not so fast that it was dangerous for swimmers. At a turn in the bayou we could see other children, diving from a thick branch of an oak overhanging the water.

For a while we stayed on the hillside, running through the peppergrass and sour dock that lined it in places. There was milkweed too, spilling white sap when we broke stalks that stood in our path, and here and there a scattering of pink wild roses. To the west an overgrown dirt road stretched like a long red ribbon through the green, leading away from the metallic glint of the bayou. Later we went diving with the other boys. They had tied a rope to the oak branch, and we took turns swinging out over the bayou and streaking in.

When the light began to fade, we rejoined Richard's father at the campsite and ate the cold cuts and salad we had brought. The chirping of the crickets, signaling the end of day, was replaced by the singing of frogs in chorus. All along the stream the melody rose; by 9 o'clock the land itself seemed to be vibrating with the sound.

Through the years, frog song has become, for me, the sound of the bayous. Only the male frog vocalizes, using his music to attract a female, and each species sings differently. One kind or another is singing year round, but the chorus is largest from March through August. In those months one hears the deep resonant hum of the bullfrog and the *quonk-quonk* of the green tree frog; the gray tree frog sends forth a sharp *brrill-brrill,* while the cricket frog emits a rattle as clear as the noise of two pebbles clicking together.

That first night I lay awake for hours, listening to the singers and watching the bayou. Bats flew, silent as shadows in the warm air above the water, searching for bugs. When the bats disappeared I wondered what other, larger nocturnal animals—bears maybe, or wildcats—might be prowling about. Richard nudged me. In the trickle of starlight that filtered down through the branches of the tree over our heads, some sort of movement was dimly visible. Something flicked from a higher branch to a lower one—not bats but flying squirrels. As my eyes adjusted to the dark, I watched them dipping and swooping gracefully—settling on one branch, skimming off to the next—a high filigree of small black patches, like pieces of the night.

Unlike bats, flying squirrels can only glide, so all their flight patterns are downward and between dives they must run back up into the trees. Their gliding apparatus is a pair of thin, furry elastic membranes attached to their sides and legs. As a squirrel launches itself into the air, it spreads out all four legs and stretches the membranes taut. Then it adjusts the slack in the membranes to control the angle and speed of a glide. At the end of its glide the squirrel pulls its hind legs together and lands upright, on all four feet; at that point the membranes relax to their original size.

The air was full of these little acrobats and their antics absorbed us until finally sleep came. About 6 o'clock the next morning, Richard shook me. His father was fixing breakfast—fish he had caught from the

*Black willows in leaf share a stand with bare cottonwoods in this aerial view of northern Louisiana bayou country. Both kinds of tree thrive best when their roots are generously watered, and are often found on river flood plains such as this nearly flat stretch along the course of a bayou.*

bank of the bayou in the light of dawn. The air was misty, and the reddish earth and gray-green country looked unreal, like a photographic image emerging in a developing solution. Fried fish reestablished reality for us, and before the sun was high we had unhitched the canoe from the top of the car, were packed up and out on the bayou.

The effects of the annual spring floods had long since gone and the bayou's water had begun to evaporate under the heat of the summer sun, so that the stream presented a kind of obstacle course. Twice we hit spots so shallow that we had to lift the canoe and portage it. The portages were places where silt had piled up sufficiently to provide a fairly firm footing. In some spots cypress trees had taken root. This happens, Richard's father explained, where the silt build-up has lasted for more than a year; and once a few of the trees get started, only a very large flood can demolish the spot—silt, cypresses and all.

By noon we had paddled to a point along the bayou where it was little more than a ditch, four feet wide. We stopped to eat lunch and enjoy a bit of shade. The sun was high and blinding, though the heat was not as bad as the kind I was accustomed to at this time of year in New Orleans; at the northern end of the state the humidity is lower, and the air relatively dry.

We were sitting, half-dozing, when my eye fell on an object about 20 yards away. It looked like a hump-shaped rock—but it was moving. It was an armadillo—a small-scale version of an armor-plated truck —heading across a patch of dry place along the bank. Armadillos are not indigenous to bayou country; native to Patagonia at the southern tip of South America, they made their way northward in a trip that probably took millions of years and did not arrive in Louisiana, according to verified sightings, until 1925. They multiply so fast—each spring producing litters of identical quadruplets—that armadillos had already become a familiar sight throughout the bayou country.

A soft plop in the bayou caught our attention next, and for a quarter hour we were entertained by a family of wood ducks. From their nest in the hollow of a tree across the stream, several baby ducks had made it into the water, a little flustered, and were paddling around busily under their mother's eye. As we watched, she began to preen. She would put her bill into the feathers at the base of her tail, then use the bill to stroke her wings and body. The duck's bill serves a dual purpose in this maneuver; it picks up the oily secretions of a gland located at the tail, then distributes the oil over the wings and body. The oil water-

Fresh from a fast bath in a woodland bayou, a wood duck ruffles the exquisitely tinted feathers that cause many ornithologists to acclaim it North America's most beautiful bird. The shy wood duck lives year round in forested bayou country and owes its name to a preference for nesting in the hollows of trees instead of on the ground.

proofs the feathers; otherwise they would become waterlogged, and the duck would be unable to fly.

Wood ducks, as their name indicates, prefer a forested habitat, and they are full-time residents of the Dorcheat. Their green and reddish-brown mix of feather colors seemed perfectly suited to the landscape.

We could have admired them for hours, but the time came to go. Richard and I ran about on a last-minute errand, filling a paper sack with the blackberries that studded bushes all around. We munched on them as the canoe took us downstream. The flow of the water was more sluggish now. As we passed a willow tree, I reached up to brush at its streamers; Mr. Breaux sharply warned me to stop. Where a bayou runs so narrow that a canoe must scrape through overhanging branches, it is a good idea to keep your hands away from things. Otherwise, you may find yourself sharing the boat with a snake, jolted by your gesture from a tree where it has gone looking for a nest of bird's eggs.

In the long afternoon we paddled through swirls of current, then through places where the water seemed not to move at all. At one place stretches of the bayou, separated by silt build-ups, were so still they were stagnant. The water on the surface looked dusty—as though it had been there for so long without moving that dirt from the banks had settled over it. The water had also begun to collect a dark green scum, and even the tree shadows looked heavier here.

A shy map turtle, five or six inches long—its olive-colored shell marked with dark lines in a geometric pattern that suggests the look of a map—slid off a log and slipped into the motionless stream. It moved quickly through the water for a few seconds, then floated head up, watchful. Beyond the turtle, an object that looked like a flowering bush stood in the high reeds. Then a leg lifted, and I saw that what I had judged to be inanimate was a great blue heron; this species, although more numerous in the southern part of the state, also nests in the northern bayous. The heron stood as quiet as if it had grown out of the mud.

The air itself seemed peculiarly still. There was a sense of secrecy about this stretch of the bayou, as though things were happening that were not visible to the eye. It was not so much the look as the feel of the place that was different.

For the next two days we continued our downstream journey. The rolling hills began to disappear; flat land was more and more frequent. Since we had only a week's time, and had to paddle all the way back upstream to our starting place, we did not try to go all the way to the end of Bayou Dorcheat at Lake Bistineau. Mr. Breaux preferred to let us stop here and there, ramble the woods and climb the trees, fish—to get to know the bayou.

During our third day out, as we were gathering kindling for our campfire, a cooing came from high in a tree above us. I watched the branches for a few minutes before I finally saw a brownish-gray bird, sitting on its nest. It was about a foot long, with a slender, pointed tail—a mourning dove. Named for its sorrowful, drawn-out call, this species of dove is common in the bayou country. While most birds nest once a year, mourning doves mate four times, producing a total of eight eggs, two at a time. For all this, the dove population does not explode, partly because the nests are flimsy platforms of grass and sticks, unprotected from winds or rainstorms or tree-climbing predators, like snakes.

The bird we were watching could have been a male or a female; both share the duties of incubating the eggs. Richard's father guessed it was a male because, he said, the male often takes the daylight shift. Suddenly, as we stood there, the dove fluttered to the ground near the trunk of the tree. It fell in an awkward way, and for a moment lay still as if stunned; then it began to flop and hobble along in a frantic effort to get as far away from us as it could. I thought its wing was broken.

Mr. Breaux merely smiled. As we headed back to the canoe, I glanced over my shoulder. The bird's entire performance had been staged to distract our attention from its nest. Now that we had gone, it pulled its wing into shape, puffed itself out like a pouter pigeon, and immediately flew back up to sit on its eggs. Such tactics are common to many species of birds that nest on the ground with their eggs vulnerable to hungry foxes, snakes and skunks. Though the mourning dove of the forested Dorcheat can nest high on branches, it has developed the same decoying technique used by its kin in the plains and deserts of other states, where doves often lay eggs among grasses or rocks. As a means of keeping the species alive, most adult doves—even tree nesters—put on their act of helplessness whenever they sense danger to their young.

Farther south on the Dorcheat, where the red rolling hills were beginning to peter out, we rounded a curve in the stream and came upon a pair of pine trees—each probably older than a century—standing higher than any of the surrounding growth. Beside the pines in one of the countless tiny tributaries of the bayou, a white sand outcropping, as white as the sand on any beach, was visible under the broken mudbank. Here in northern Louisiana, some 40 million years ago, had been the ancient coast of the Gulf of Mexico. The sand remained as a tes-

The stands of pine and hardwood trees that line the edges of northern bayous provide a meeting ground for four wild flowers that separately thrive in very different habitats elsewhere. Grass-pink orchids abound in bogs; jewelweed, also called touch-me-not for the way its seed pods burst open when touched, flourishes in marshes; the low-growing Carolina mallow often invades lawns, and spiderwort does as well in dry pinelands as in the moist soil near the bayous.

GRASS-PINK ORCHID

JEWELWEED

CAROLINA MALLOW

SPIDERWORT

tament to that time, and to the millions of streams that had appeared and disappeared, building up land southward into a wilderness of silt, water and green growth.

Several hundred yards beyond the two pines, the woods lay peaceful and quiet. Mr. Breaux drove the canoe in to shore. After we had prowled through the woods for an hour or so, he declared resttime, and we sat down in a clearing. But we were soon bored and restive, and Richard's father came up with another diversion. He raised his hands to his mouth, cupped them together, uttered a long, clear, plaintive cry, then lowered his hands. We waited, mystified. Nothing happened.

He was imitating the sound of a wild-turkey hen seeking a mate; it is not an easy cry to duplicate. Wild turkeys are famous for their keen hearing. A caller not only has to be accurate in the sound he makes, but must remain totally silent once he has made it. In springtime—the turkeys' mating season—the call of a single female wishing to join a tom turkey's harem carries for a great distance in the woods. On hearing it, a male will seek her out, strut, and spread his feathers. Even after the season, the hen's call may attract a curious male.

Mr. Breaux repeated the call twice more. But the quiet was broken only by the rustling of a breeze in the branches high above us and by the hard cry of a distant blue jay. I opened my mouth to say something. Mr. Breaux held a finger to his lips. The precaution struck me as silly, but I settled back.

Again he made the call; again there was no answer. My left leg was falling asleep, and I couldn't move without making some noise because I was sitting on a bed of dry leaves. I inched one knee up slowly. Richard's father frowned at me, and I decided to speak up whether he liked it or not; I was about to, when I saw something move over his shoulder, 20 yards behind him.

In the space between two red-oak trees, a big and powerful-looking tom turkey was scratching at the ground. Then he began to strut. Richard pointed, and his father nodded. So slowly that the movement was almost imperceptible, Mr. Breaux began to turn his head and shoulders. The tom, which had not seen us, stopped and looked around. Like many novice woodsmen under similar circumstances, I developed an immediate and overpowering desire to sneeze. I tried to control myself, but only partially succeeded, making a low, choked sound. The tom melted into the underbrush and disappeared from sight.

Richard's father looked at me hopelessly, and made the call again. For what seemed hours we waited in the clearing, and then another tom turkey appeared. He was larger than the first one, more deliberate in his movements. With a sort of slow-motion strut, he passed within 10 yards of where we sat and continued on into the underbrush.

That clearing was as far south as we went on the Dorcheat. Late that afternoon Mr. Breaux decided that we should begin the more difficult return trip upstream. After three days, we hoisted the canoe back onto the top of the car and left Louisiana's northern hills behind us.

I was not to see a bayou as wild as the Dorcheat for another three years. When I was 13, I had a look at a very different part of the bayou country under the guidance of my own father. This time there were no hills, no rolling country. The land was as flat as it is in New Orleans, and the trip much shorter than the way to the Dorcheat—a distance of no more than 100 miles. We headed southwest from the city on open country roads, past pale earth that seemed to grow darker and wetter as we traveled. Hackberry trees (called sugarberries in other states) were heavy with the sweet reddish fruit that Louisiana birds favor; live oaks were interspersed with the hackberries along the roadside. The white oaks I had seen rising 70 to 80 feet above the Dorcheat would have towered over these live oaks, no one of which could have been more than 40 feet tall. But what the live oaks lacked in height they made up for in breadth—stretching out their branches to make crowns 100 feet or more across. Both the deciduous white oaks and the related, but evergreen, live oaks bear acorns; but while the leaves of the white oak are deep lobed, paper thin and shaped like open hands, those of the live oak are oval, leathery textured and smooth edged.

The streams nearby were muddy, the color of milk chocolate, as if the earth had melted and begun to ooze. The clamshell roads over which we drove were white and dusty. Near the Gulf, clam and sometimes oyster shells—because they are plentiful, weigh less than gravel and are easier to haul—are used to surface everything from private driveways to secondary roads. The shells are dredged, mainly from Lake Pontchartrain, by machines that operate like giant vacuum cleaners. After the shells are deposited and spread in place, they are crushed with rollers. The bits compact quickly into a roadbed that is firm, but still resilient enough to flex with the jelly-like land beneath.

Finally we stopped at a broad stream; I got out of the car and walked up onto a levee to look down at the dark water. Lines of live oaks drooped and patches of long yellow spiked cane and green palmettos reared up from the banks like oversized hands, motionless in the shade of the trees. Waxlike leaves shone wetly, and the stream shone through them into darkness.

We were on Bayou Teche, the most elegant of all the bayous; though itself too civilized to be considered wilderness, it borders some of the least-traveled swamps of the Atchafalaya Basin. Originating near Port Barre, in the south-central part of the state, the Teche meanders south and east for more than 100 miles, curling lazily back and forth until it finally spills into Berwick Bay near the Gulf of Mexico.

Legend has it that a silver snake of fabulous proportions once terrorized the region of the Teche. When Indian warriors set out to kill the snake, they rained arrows into its body, and after they ran out of arrows used clubs on it. In its death agony the serpent cut huge grooves into the soil, which later became filled with water. The stream was known by the local Indian word for snake, *tenche*, which eventually was modified to Teche.

In the northern part of the Teche there is a long stretch of about 50 miles where the bayou is only 100 feet or so wide. Where we were walking, near its southernmost end, the bayou is twice as broad as that. On the opposite levee, we could make out clusters of dark green ferns and tall trees thickened with gray Spanish moss. The water between the banks ran slowly, dark and warm-looking under the sun. In the dusky light that pervades the Teche whatever the time of day, there are always shadows.

For the next days my father and I followed small bayous westward from the Teche through countryside that grew more and more wild-looking. A stream would go sometimes in one direction, sometimes in another; one led into a waterway so small it could hardly be called a bayou, then into a marshy spot that turned back into a larger stream. We didn't know where we were going, and yet it was as if the long walks were leading to some particular end. Anyone who has hiked through this wilderness has known the feeling. It is as if the streams are drawing you into a whirlpool of smaller and smaller circles, spiraling inward to a deep center that pulls you almost against your will.

One morning my father allowed me to wander off alone. Clumps of thorny dewberry bushes sprawled over the ground here and there, and I had to go around them. In doing so I changed direction many times, and by the time the sun was high I knew that I was lost. The streams I followed had an almost mesmerizing quality; the sluggish tempo of the bayou flow had taken over. The plants I saw seemed to grow faster than the streams themselves moved.

Once a small bird led me across a patch of clover-leaved wood sorrel through high grass to a stand of hackberry and magnolia trees. The magnolias were in full bloom, their scent so strong as to be almost overpowering. Within the dark green leaves the white blossoms seemed to be bursting. The sun was so bright I couldn't look up toward the sky for very long. Then the magnolias were behind me and I came upon a small stream. I veered to avoid stepping into it and found what I had been drawn to all along.

The end of the journey was a nameless place, a kind of arch of shadows. I stopped and looked around. Oaks and willows and cypresses on either side of the stream formed an interlocking fan above it. The water was motionless, dark brown, and the moss and leaves overhead nearly blotted out the sky. Tall reeds, a few jack-in-the-pulpits and wild dandelions lined the mudbanks. Something in the reeds stirred—a swamp rabbit. It looked at me, then calmly went back to munching.

There was a stillness, an airlessness about this place, as if the whole earth were holding its breath. Then without warning, a darkness fell. It happened so fast that for a moment I thought I had gone to sleep on my feet and lost track of time. A single wide, black shadow had blotted out the sun; the tops of the tree branches looked as though a pair of gigantic wings were hovering over them. Then there was a far-off lightning flash of dim white. Before the thunder could follow it, rain started to rattle through the leaves. Big warm drops sloped onto the earth from the black cloud above. The rain was gentle, and the dark was somehow comforting.

NATURE WALK / **Exploring the Dorcheat**

PHOTOGRAPHS BY ROBERT WALCH

At first glance, the Dorcheat gave every appearance of being a typical bayou. Its waters were moving slowly, even after several days of heavy spring rain, and ranks of bald cypress, sweet gum, water oak and other hardwoods crowded its banks. Yet an element classically associated with bayous was missing: no Spanish moss draped the branches of the cypresses. For the Dorcheat is a northern bayou.

Like other northern bayous, the Dorcheat, which rises in Arkansas and flows down into northwestern Louisiana, differs in three distinct ways from bayous in the south: it has better drainage, the atmosphere is less humid and the climate is cooler. As a result, there is less swamp area—although in spring the Dorcheat has its share—and the vegetation is not so lush. The curious thing is that none of this should affect Spanish moss. It could grow perfectly well in the northern part of the state, but for some unexplained reason only an occasional trace of it grows along the Dorcheat.

From a clearing at the bayou's edge that afforded a good view of its dark waters both upstream and down, the trail plunged into thick woods and then led upstream for about eight miles to a bridge near the Arkansas border. This part of the Dorcheat runs through a land of cattle ranches, lumbered forests and oil wells, but the river's array of animal life and its brooding, timeless aura made the human enterprises out of sight beyond the next ridge easy to escape—and forget.

Along the way this special quality of isolation was enhanced by the weather. All morning, thick spring rain clouds kept sweeping in to hang over the Dorcheat for a few moments, softening the greenery, scattering a few large drops of rain and briefly shutting off the rest of the world before being blown away by crisp gusts of wind. Then the bayou and its protective greenery would brighten in a wash of sunlight.

The thick woods along the bayou were loud with morning activity. Woodpeckers drummed their energetic beat as they drilled nest holes in live trees and combed dead trunks for meals of bark beetles, wood borers and termites. Two red-headed woodpeckers broke into a brief, furious fight; one paid for violating the territory of the other by being driven across the bayou. Overhead a turkey buzzard wheeled on the air currents, its crimson head sharply

*HARDWOODS AT THE DORCHEAT'S EDGE*

visible even at a distance. Also riding the currents was a pair of red-shouldered hawks. The hawks do very well for themselves at this time of year: the spring floods force many small creatures out of their natural cover onto ground where they are more vulnerable to aerial attack.

On the bank of the bayou stood a

*BIRDHOUSES IN A CYPRESS*

straight old bald cypress whose partially hollowed-out trunk was doing double duty as a riverside housing project. Half a dozen tiered holes in the tree, originally drilled by woodpeckers, were now being claimed as summer homes by other birds, perhaps several kinds, although on this morning only a couple of starlings were to be seen flitting in and out of their high-rise dwellings.

The old cypress made an admirable apartment house. During the scores of years it had grown beside the bayou, its leafy crown had been broken, probably a number of times, by lightning strikes or hurricanes. Exposed to the rain and weather, the interior of the trunk rotted, softened and slowly disintegrated from the top down. The tree did not die, how-

A SHY SLIDER TURTLE

ever, since nourishment is carried to the growing parts through the trunk's outer layers. In fact the hollow trunk may have actually saved the life of the cypress by causing it to be passed over by the loggers who scour the Dorcheat in search of valuable lumber.

On a sun-dappled log a slider turtle snoozed serenely in the warmth of midday. It must have been there for a while as its head and legs were tucked into the shell; basking turtles do this when a hot sun begins to dry their skin out. Alarmed by a rustle somewhere in the brush, the turtle flipped deftly into the water and swam off.

The trail led deeper into the woods, and suddenly there was plenty of water around—but no river. The spring rains had sent the Dor-

A BELL-BOTTOMED BALD CYPRESS

cheat over its low-lying banks to inundate the flood plain; for miles around, hardwoods and pines rose spectrally from the calm, reflecting waters. Why was this section of the Dorcheat flooded, while downstream —and upstream too, as it turned out later in the day—the waters were contained by the banks?

Even at its swiftest, the Dorcheat never courses rapidly. It drops only about 80 feet in the 50-odd miles from the Arkansas border to Lake Bistineau just above the Red River —a descent so gradual that the bayou never builds up enough speed or power to gouge a very deep channel. But in some places, as here, a few miles south of the Arkansas border, the land is so flat the Dorcheat has practically no channel to deepen. It slows to a crawl and deposits much of its silt load. In the drier months the shallow sections of the riverbed become mud flats that require boatmen to portage their craft to the next stretch of water. But when spring rains swell the river, the portages are covered and the waters spread over the banks to creep into the forests. There they remain until the sun dries the land.

Of all the trees rising from the flood plain, the bald cypress appeared the most at home. With its huge, bell-bottomed trunk and enigmatic knees sticking up from its root system, the cypress is traditionally associated with warm, watery locales. By comparison, the loblolly pines seemed out of place, standing with the bottoms of their trunks temporarily concealed in the brown

water. Not as massive or majestic as the bald cypress, the loblolly pine nevertheless has its own grace as it rises 80 feet straight up.

The source of the name loblolly is as convoluted as the pine is straight. The word has a variety of meanings: in one sense, it is a kind of thick

*A FLOODED LOBLOLLY*

gruel, in another it betokens a loutish fellow, and in North Carolina it is used to describe a natural damp depression in the land where this particular type of pine prospers because its roots tolerate wet soil better than most pines.

The species is not limited to North Carolina, however, nor to damp ground. It is a relentless colonizer, a sort of weed among pines that thrives wherever its seeds can reach bare soil—particularly abandoned, burned or cutover fields. Because of this capacity for growing in neglected land, the loblolly has become one of the most common of the eastern evergreens. It is cut for lumber and cultivated for the manufacture of paper. Close examination of a low loblolly branch revealed the reason for the tree's ability to proliferate: a cluster of young male cones heavy with pollen. With the onset of summer, the cones would wither and fall off, but not before the wind had distributed the pollen widely to fertilize female cones.

The climb became steeper as a red clay ridge rose beside the Dorcheat's flood plain. Here the lower limbs of the loblolly pines were sparse. In the shade, deprived of sunlight, limbs die and fall off, in a kind of self-pruning. Only the upper branches

*POLLEN-RICH PINE CONES*

*A RIDGETOP STAND OF LOBLOLLY*

get enough sunlight to stay alive.

The seedlings of sweet gum and other hardwoods that were infiltrating the pine stand are not so choosy about sunlight. In time these tiny trees will carpet the entire floor below the pines, in shade where the pines' own seedlings have trouble surviving; the hardwoods will grow and win the competition for light. As they tower and spread their leafy branches, they will eventually triumph decisively over the pines.

Not only do the pines self-prune without sunlight, they also, in effect, self-destruct without it.

Ridges like this one were formed in an indirect way by the Mississippi River. As the silt it dumped built up the delta in the south, the weight of those deposits exerted tremendous pressure on the earth's crust. Like a massive seesaw, the land mass of northern Louisiana reacted to the weight in the south with an uplift, a geological phenomenon that formed the ridges and hills. The fulcrum for this seesaw is just above the capital of Baton Rouge in the south-central part of the state.

At the top of the ridge the sunlight glinted suddenly on the shiny green armor of a tiger beetle that was hurtling with flying leaps across the forest floor. The tiger beetle is a favorite of farmers and gardeners, not because of its handsome carapace but because it is an efficient enemy of various insect pests, such as the destructive gypsy moth. The little tiger beetles are downright voracious, in fact, and will attack creatures as large as snails.

TIGER BEETLE

COACHWHIP

MULLEIN PLANT

For a moment it even looked as though this beetle were about to tackle a snake; one long hop landed it right next to an eastern coachwhip coiled elegantly on a bed of dry pine needles. But neither creature showed any interest in the other. The beetle zoomed on its erratic course, and the snake continued to bask in the sun.

It is said that the coachwhip will curl itself around the leg of a man and whip him to death with its tail. Not true. Actually, the snake gets its name from the intricate pattern of scales that gives it an uncanny resemblance to a braided leather whip. The whiplike motion of the tail as the snake moves reinforces the name —and the legend. But rather than whipping, the snake depends for its defense primarily on protective coloration and speed.

Even so, this coachwhip caused one unnerving moment before it finally glided out of sight; its quivering tail tip struck some dead leaves and produced a sound exactly like the rattle of a diamondback.

Also getting the most from the sun was a mullein, an unassuming plant with a clump of soft, velvety leaves. In midsummer this prosaic plant sends forth a tall spike, one to two feet high, from which will bloom clusters of small yellow flowers. Mullein is a home remedy; the tea brewed from its leaves is much acclaimed as a relief for respiratory ailments. The plant also served a purpose in the days before commercially packaged rouge. When the hairy leaves were rubbed on the pale cheeks of local belles, they stimulated the blood to flow and produced a modestly lingering blush.

The trail eventually led over the red clay ridge and back down into the hardwood-dominated lowlands. The floodwaters still made it impossible to tell where the real bayou was —a shallow green pool lay in a depression among the trees. But already the spring sun was drying up the water, and in a few weeks the leaf-strewn floor would be dry again.

On a log in the forest a little cotton mouse was resting, with the haggard look of a creature that has endured many hardships. And well it might have. For during this time of flooding, all creatures, including snakes and mice, are driven into the narrowing dry zones together. With their hunting ranges reduced by the waters, the snakes are in keen competition for the mice. The mice thus live in extra jeopardy, and must be especially alert to survive.

There certainly seemed to be a lot of snakes about. In short order two more appeared—first a harmless black rat snake, then a young but deadly copperhead. As the name implies, the rat snake is a consumer of rodents; this one, initially drawn by the cotton mouse, now found it was confronted and cornered by a human enemy. Like the coachwhip, its tail vibrating among some dead leaves, the rat snake sent out an ominous —but meaningless—rattle. It lunged forward, mouth open in a display of ferocity, but the show was temporary; it moved off smoothly into the underbrush. Also like the coachwhip, the speedy rat snake is a

BAYOU OVERFLOW IN THE WOODS

nimble climber, and is likely to make its nest in made-to-order cavities of high, hollow trees.

The copperhead blended so perfectly into the background of dead leaves that only a trained eye could have spotted it from more than a few feet away. Camouflage is one of its defenses, but poison is its heavy artillery—it belongs to the same group as the rattlesnake and cottonmouth. The copperhead is known as the highland moccasin while the cottonmouth is called the water moccasin.

Copperheads are night feeders, generally lethargic by day, and this one lay coiled in its defensive posture without striking out. A trace of yellow on its tail indicated that the snake was slightly more than a year old. For the first year, the copperhead's tail is a greenish yellow, which then slowly disappears. The snake endured a cautious inspection and then, after some defensive pos-

COTTON MOUSE

DOGWOOD IN FLOWER

turing, executed a graceful retreat.

Even in the shade the late morning was warm, particularly when the breezes languished, but the dimness and humidity were evidently just right for a flowering dogwood tree, which illuminated the woods with a pastel display of tiny yellow flowers centered in symmetrical white petal-like bracts. Dogwood is an exceptional plant in that it can carry on normal photosynthesis at one third full sunlight. While other plants wither and the growth of other trees is stifled in the shade, the dogwood thrives as though it were drenched in full sunlight.

For some time the way had led through forest and flooded woods that denied a view of the Dorcheat itself. But now, just beyond a thick patch of saplings and underbrush, the bayou reappeared, flowing serenely once again within the limits of its regular channel. A perfume

COPPERHEAD

RAT SNAKE

came wafting on the wind from a tall bush of wild azalea. Honeybees were seeking the sweet nectar from its upper branches. The blossoms of the wild azalea are so fragrant, the taste of them so sweet, that it is known locally as honeysuckle, even though it is quite different from the vine plant of the same name.

WILD AZALEA

The drooping blooms of a young wild-black-cherry tree also enlivened the bayou's edge. If it grows in a field away from the competition of the forest, the wild black cherry usually has a stubby trunk and knotty branches. But in the woods, competing for light with other trees, it may rise to a height of 100 feet with a trunk five feet in diameter.

A long, low bridge spanning the Dorcheat marked the walk's end. A county road crossed the bayou by way of the bridge, and cultivated land lay beyond the ridge on the other side. Noisily confirming the nearness of human enterprise, a farm pickup truck suddenly rattled over the bridge, its driver unmindful of the bayou. Civilization had intruded abruptly and shattered the mood of the time and the place.

BLACK-CHERRY BLOSSOMS

Yet as the dust of the vehicle's passing settled, the warm, sunny midday grew still again. The bridge afforded a wide view of the bayou and the thick stands of hardwoods along both banks. A twisted, dead branch jutted from the water, causing only the faintest disturbance in the gentle current. The bayou's wildness slowly reestablished itself; and, as if for emphasis, a woodpecker drummed its tattoo against a tree in the deep woods not 50 yards away.

*THE VIEW FROM THE BRIDGE*

# 3/ Hurricane in the Atchafalaya

*Then the Wind grew weird. It ceased being a breath;
it became a Voice moaning across the world — hooting —
uttering nightmare sounds.* LAFCADIO HEARN/ CHITA

It was years after my trips to Bayou Dorcheat and Bayou Teche, during a humid week in late summer, that I discovered the region I came to think of as quintessential bayou country, and encountered the storm responsible for giving that area a justified reputation as a place of danger —hurricane country.

Hurricane is a word that means little to those who have not seen at least the edge of such a storm. We read in the newspapers that a hurricane has struck some coast, done so many dollars' worth of damage, and passed on. Perhaps a few lives have been lost—perhaps more than a few. Often 25-foot-high storm swells, started out at sea by the winds, have raced the hurricane to the coast and are reported to have caused more havoc than the storm itself. The story appears in the papers one day, two or three at most, then is gone as the storm is gone and we think no more about it.

In New Orleans, with the Gulf Coast and hurricane country nearby, the word is a more familiar one, and a few facts accumulate around it through the years. I remembered, for instance, hearing that the great hurricane that struck Florida on Labor Day in 1935 killed 150 people and did six million dollars' worth of damage. In science class at school I learned something about how our own Louisiana hurricanes are believed to form: over the mid-Atlantic near the equator in summer, two winds coming from opposite directions may meet and start to twirl around each other in a counterclockwise motion that is accentuated by the forces of the earth's rotation. Hot moist air from the ocean beneath the winds is drawn up into the center. As this air rises and cools, its moisture condenses and throws off heat that releases extra energy into the rotating mass, making it rise and spin even faster. As more and more tropical sea air sweeps in to replace the rising air, condensation quickens to create thunderclouds around the core, or eye, of the towering ring-shaped storm. It becomes an official, full-fledged hurricane, I learned, when its internal winds reach a speed of 74 mph. Meantime the storm has started to move northwest at about 10 mph, gathering momentum and intensity.

Usually hurricanes never hit land at all, but blow themselves out at sea. When they do come ashore they can hit anywhere from the West Indies to New England; occasionally they thread their way across the Gulf of Mexico to strike Louisiana. As a schoolboy I knew that the official hurricane season for southern Louisiana begins the first of June and ends the 30th of November, and that the peak of the season is during the month of September.

Yet statistics such as these never quite take on reality. They remain as remote as a set of old road maps tucked into a cupboard. And so, when a high-school classmate asked me, one hot August, to join him for a week of fishing in the Atchafalaya swamp, I jumped at the chance. I knew there was a hurricane brewing in the Gulf, everybody did—it had been announced in the papers and over the radio—but if it struck shore at all, it was expected to hit south and west of where we were going. The enormous swamp filling the 75-mile-long Atchafalaya River Basin, which I had long wanted to explore, was nowhere near the course the storm was taking; besides, I had never heard of a storm, even a bad one, doing much damage to a place like that. The fact that a hurricane can alter its course several times in a single day didn't disturb me because I didn't know about it. Nor did I consider that storm damage to uninhabited swampland is not reported in detail for a very simple reason—no one is there to report it.

I wedged the butt of a fishing rod into a duffel bag with some old clothes, a few cans of food and a thermos of coffee, and stood on a street corner in the French Quarter of New Orleans waiting for Jim to pick me up. It was 4 o'clock in the morning; like all fishermen we wanted to get an early start. The sky was deep blue-black, the air heavy with heat, and nothing seemed further away than danger of any kind. When Jim pulled up in an old truck, I hopped in and we took off across the bridge to the other side of the Mississippi River, heading west.

In little over an hour and a half we reached what Jim called his parents' hunting lodge. A few hundred yards from the banks of a bayou, it was one of a small group of jerry-built shacks owned by city families who used them as bases from which to go fishing and frogging and crawfishing and crabbing, and to shoot squirrel and rabbit and deer. We arrived before dawn, but after one look at the line of trucks already waiting to launch boats from the makeshift dock at the water's edge, we decided to spend the day some other way and go fishing the next morning when we could get an even earlier start.

After we got the truck unpacked and made some breakfast, we turned on the radio in the shack. A news announcer said that the hurricane, still in the Gulf, was moving forward at 15 mph in a northwesterly direction, and was expected to hit the low-lying Louisiana coastal areas, not far from the Texas border, by nightfall. We turned the radio off and thought no more about it.

We spent most of the day enjoying the bird songs in the trees around us. There were dozens of warblers, among them the prothonotary warbler—a beautiful bird no larger than a canary, with slate-blue wings and a bright yellow head and breast. Jim spotted an indigo bunting, and I a painted bunting, its gaudily colored body lashed indiscriminately with rose red, yellow-green and violet blue, as if paint had been thrown at it by a drunken artist.

The gray moss overhead fascinated us too, trailing in places for more than a yard, touching the ground or the surface of the water. This moss has become so closely identified with bayous that it is a kind of symbol of them. There is something moody and dark, a sense of brooding, about its gray presence in the pervasive green. The rival French and Spanish explorers who came to this wilderness both marveled at the moss, and vied with one another in attempting to name it. The story is that the French called it, somewhat derisively, *barbe espagnole,* Spanish beard; the Spaniards countered by dubbing it *peluca francesa,* or Frenchman's wig. The French won out and today it is known as Spanish moss; its scientific name is *Tillandsia usneoides.*

Local Indian legend—which has an explanation for most things found in the bayou country—tells of a girl killed by an enemy tribe during her wedding ceremony. Her mourning family cut off her hair and spread it on the limbs of the oak tree under which she was buried. The hair then blew from tree to tree, finally turning gray, and it endures as a tribute to those who are not fated to live out their love. The facts are less ro-

Outside its nest hole in a charred tree stump, a prothonotary warbler prepares to digest its catch. An annual warm-weather visitor to Louisiana from Central America, the warbler was named by local Creoles for the yellow-garbed prothonotaries who are prelates of the Roman Catholic Church.

mantic. Botanically, Spanish moss is not a true moss; it is a member of the pineapple family and is epiphytic—nourished by air. It isn't a parasite, as is commonly believed, nor does it smother the trees it lives in. It can grow just as well in dead trees as in live ones, for it feeds only on dust carried through it by breezes. It bears tiny emerald-green flowers, like minute lilies, that cannot be seen from more than a few yards away, but carry cylindrical seed pods. The parent plant reproduces not only by seeding but also by breaking off when swayed by winds; bits of moss landing on other branches continue to grow at a steady rate, averaging about an inch a month.

Through the years Spanish moss has been gathered for many uses. The Indians clothed their infants in it, used it to bolster their reed-and-mud huts, and even claimed to cure illness with it. A sick man would be wrapped in many layers of the moss and laid on a high cane bed set over a charcoal fire topped by boiling herbs. The vapors and heat rising through the moss produced a heavy sweat in the patient, which was believed to rid his system of disease.

Jim and I spent that first evening listening to the bayou frog chorus. The green frog, locally known as the banjo frog because its voice rattles like a loose banjo string, was most conspicuous among the other croakers. One green frog sat motionless and silent at the base of a hackberry tree as we watched—its tongue darting in and out for bugs so fast that we were unaware of the movement until a delicate shimmering dragonfly, caught on the wing, lay folded and crushed in the frog's small green jaws.

We went to sleep very early and woke four hours after midnight to make breakfast and load the family's fishing yacht (an old rowboat aided by a rusty outboard motor) onto a platform on wheels that hooked to the back of the truck. While we were working, a man from a neighboring shack came by and told us of the latest radio announcement. The hurricane had veered off course and had struck the Gulf Coast earlier than expected; it was southwest of us, but no official warning had been given to evacuate our area. Still, it was best to be on the safe side, the neighbor added—you could never tell about a hurricane.

Jim and I decided not to stay out in the bayous longer than half a day. If the hurricane were to head anywhere near our vicinity, which seemed unlikely, noon would be time enough to get out of its way. While hurricane winds have been known to rise to 200 mph, the forward movement of the hurricane itself is rarely much faster than 15 to

20 mph. The storm was now almost 150 miles off, and there seemed no reason not to go fishing.

We drove the truck to the dock along a road lined with magnolia trees. A thick black predawn sky was paling slowly at the edges to ash-blue; overhead it was heavily overcast, like a dark sagging roof above the land. The air, even though sunup was an hour away, was fevered with summer. On the southwest horizon the sky briefly gleamed now and then with the ominous, soundless glow of heat lightning. The mist was heavy enough to require the use of windshield wipers. At the landing—a small area of earth packed with white clamshells—the rank metallic smell of the water was mixed with the fresh smell of live fish and the sweet scents of honeysuckle and verbena. We were early enough this time to beat the crowd. In 10 minutes we were on the water headed for the center of the swamp, with the outboard motor chugging comfortably at the stern. Other small fishing boats took off from the landing and disappeared quickly in the distance. The fish we were out to catch—green trout, sac-a-lait, bream—were in the small bayous that intertwined the large swamp to our west. Actually, fishing merely gave our excursion a purpose; what we really wanted was to see the swamp without parental guidance.

Above us now the trees were becoming loud with bird song. The birds were noisier than usual, we decided, because of the cloudy weather. The far bank was lined with cypress and willow trees. Jim headed between them into a stream that led away at a right angle from the one we were on; we followed it for about half a mile, then took a smaller stream that forked off, then another fork that branched from that, then still another. Soon we were in a maze of quiet small bayous—meandering streams that seemed to lead nowhere. The dawn was coming fast, the sky clogged with clouds, an occasional break of misty blue showing through like pale smoke. High in the east, a lone heron streaked silently over the swamp. We came to another narrow stream and Jim took it. Then he turned the motor off, and let the skiff drift.

Without the chugging of the engine, in the sudden silence, we felt uneasy. Neither of us made any move to take out a fishing rod. I noticed that Jim pressed the palms of his hands over his ears and released them twice, as if to test his hearing ability. I heard nothing. The silence lay about us like a sleep. We avoided each other's eyes and sat drifting, saying nothing. The skiff moved more slowly, finally coming to a stop, poised over the stream.

A haze over an eerily still bayou, caused by moisture build-up in high-altitude clouds, heralds a change in the weather, possibly a storm.

The silence in a cypress swamp seems, oddly, to contain some mysterious sound. It is as if all the small ordinary noises of day were removed to make the ear ready for something else—something that can almost be heard, but not quite. Jim and I sat, straining our ears, focusing our attention on the thing we only sensed was there. All around us ripples in the water glided outward from the skiff and broke soundlessly on the mud embankments. Then some ordinary noises seemed to come back, but from a distance. A red-winged blackbird called a few raucous notes from a nearby branch, but the bird, and the branch too, seemed somehow removed from us.

Of its own accord the skiff began to move again slowly. We passed a line of water-ash trees arrayed like friendly ghosts on the bank. Jim ducked to avoid an overhanging branch, its tip supporting a small brownish wasp's nest. Alongside the boat, minuscule insects made dents and streaks in the water without ever breaking its surface. A sudden patch of mosquitoes zoomed past and slipped into the silence. Palmettos bent forward, their flat-fingered leaves limp in the heavy air. The skiff drifted, then stopped again, its bow nuzzling a knotty cypress "knee" that jutted out of the stream.

Cypress, the most abundant tree in Louisiana swamps, has an odd look: it appears to be waiting for some unforeseeable event. The tree before us, its feathery deep-green leaves punctuated by gray moss, stood like a mourner in readiness, seeming to be supported by the knees, which rose from its roots. Whether the knees do actually help the tree stand firm in its base of muck is not certain. There are various other theories as to their function—that they are exposed in order to increase the tree's intake of oxygen, or that they serve to store nutriments for it. Whatever the reason for the knees, the cypress seems indestructible. In this part of the world its lumber is known as wood eternal.

The bow of the skiff drifted off the cypress knee and we moved on, passing more cypresses and other trees as well—sweet gum, persimmon, water locust—their branches and leaves mingled in a canopy overhead. A gray squirrel, called a cat squirrel here, ran along a branch of a tupelo-gum tree and hurdled the stream, landing on a tree on the opposite bank. Yellow-throated warblers filtered from nests built on bunches of Spanish moss high in the tips of the branches, out of reach of all but the most intrepid of snakes.

The sky had taken on a gray, bloated look; it was a single mass of clouds swollen with light, almost too bright to look at without squinting. Jim turned his head, and I followed his glance. High up on the bank to our left lay the wreck of a skiff like ours. Only its skeleton hull and a few boards with rusty nails remained, a testament to some long-past surge of wind and water that had lifted and deposited it so far out of the stream. Jim and I decided not to fish today, but instead just tour for a while. Jim started the motor again and we turned back to one of the wider streams behind us. The main bayou—the one we had taken at our first turn—had divided and redivided so many times it was impossible to tell whether we were headed north or south, east or west. We should have brought a compass, but had neglected to do so; now we would have to rely on our general sense of direction.

It is easy to get lost in the Atchafalaya. In fact, it is a rash idea to go in at all without a guide who is so familiar with each bend and turn that he can travel in his sleep. To the two of us, 17 years old and un-initiated, one stream looked like another; we recognized the main bayou, when we finally reached it, only because of its size. A few cottonwoods and sycamores grew here along with the cypresses, and the earth itself had a verdant look. The bayou water, too, was greenish, re-flecting trees like a mirror image of the swamp life above. To check our depth, Jim dug an oar upright into the water. Halfway down it stuck in mud. The soil lay only a little way beneath the surface of the water just as water lurked only a little way beneath the surface of the earth that supported the trees. The swamp was neither solid nor liquid, earth nor water, but a thickened mixture of both.

The light in the sky had grown grayer. Two great blue herons streaked by; in the darkening morning their wings appeared to brush the tree-tops. Then a peal of thunder sounded. The next moment a few raindrops dotted the water. I felt some on my arms and the back of my neck. Jim poled the skiff beneath the protective branches of a cypress. Neither of us minded the rain; it seemed a part of things in this wilderness. Not just water and earth, but water, earth and sky were one around us —like the roots and trunk and leaves of a single tree. We watched as the rain increased from a mass of dots to a solid sheet. Jim glanced up at the cypress branches. So far, the leaves were shielding us relatively well; we knew, though, that if the squall lasted more than 15 minutes or so, the cypress would no longer provide any protection. But rain-storms in the swamp rarely last long; they come and go with each pass-ing cloud. The trouble was, the cloud above us could not pass. It covered the entire sky. The word "hurricane" was in our minds by now, though neither of us had spoken it aloud.

Half an hour later the rain was cascading down on our heads; our high boots were full and sloshing, our clothes clinging to our bodies. Jim pointed over my shoulder in the general direction of the clamshell dock from which we had set out. I nodded, and he started the motor and aimed the skiff into the center of the bayou. Water was rising in the bottom of the boat; I took a can and began to bail as Jim steered. Despite the summer heat, the rain felt cold, and we shivered. Ahead, the streaks of water were so thick it was impossible to see more than a few yards. Another fishing skiff loomed out of the rain and veered off to our port side. As it passed, Jim yelled, "Are you going in?" The two men in the other boat, both covered in yellow slickers, nodded. Without another word, Jim reversed direction; we turned in a tight arc and began to follow them. Then we looked at each other and laughed. If the men had not come along it would have been nothing to laugh about; we had been going the wrong way—deeper into the swamp rather than out of it.

Following in the wake of the other skiff, we relaxed and the unspoken fear we had felt turned to an exhilaration close to euphoria. Jim began to yodel under the cascading sheets of water. I joined in. We did not know that the squall, bad as it seemed to be, was only one of the small cloudbursts that sometimes precede a dangerous tropical storm; we did not know that the front edge of the hurricane, which had changed direction again, now lay only about a hundred miles to the south of us. The storm was approaching the swamp in an unerring straight line. The skiff chugged along merrily, and the branches on either bank of the bayou dipped and swayed in the pelting water as if the trees were bowing to us. The place felt safe. The look of it was extraordinary. The vast mist of the Atchafalaya rose all around us like steam, monochrome and thick, heavy and wet.

We docked at the landing, dripping and shivering, almost three hours before our noon deadline. As we maneuvered the boat onto the trailer, an old fisherman next to us wiped the streaming water out of his eyes with the back of his wrist, looked up at the gray glare of the sky, and shook his head. "You all better get out of here fast," he said, without looking at us, in the voice of a man who has spent much of his life trying, vainly, to cope with the idiosyncrasies of city folk. I said the storm didn't look that bad. "Storm?" he said, "this ain't no storm." The old man looked straight at me; his pale eyes flashed like a fish coming to the surface of the water. "You all better get out of here," he said again, in a firm, low tone. Then he turned and walked up the landing.

Back at the shack, Jim and I took off our wet clothes and rubbed ourselves down with towels. We put on dry jeans and sweaters and brewed some coffee on the ancient stove to warm us. Outside, the rain was still coming down—no slower, no faster. I told Jim what the old fisherman had said, and he scoffed. "Uncle of mine has a summer house about fifty miles northwest of here," he said, "big enough to hold up under any storm. He'll put us up if we want. If the hurricane comes, we can watch it from the house . . . maybe go out in it." I said I wondered whether we ought to chance driving there. "Hell," Jim said, swallowing a smile, "if you're chicken. . . ." I rose and packed my things quickly, and we locked the front door and ran out to the truck. Jim started the motor and we headed up a dirt road that led northwest. About 25 miles on, the rain suddenly ceased. Jim glanced in my direction and grinned. "See?" he said, cocksure. "I told you."

After three more dirt roads and another hour, we turned onto a clamshell driveway flanked by hackberry and live-oak trees. This part of the swamp country was heavily wooded; we had seen no other building of any kind for the last 20 miles. As we pulled up under the branches of a big oak near the garage I saw a glint of dark water beyond the trees on the far side of the house where the place bordered the eastern edge of the swamp. Jim went up to the door and rang the bell while I stood in the driveway and watched the sky. Its harsh, blinding look had given way to a glow that pulsated through the unending bank of clouds. The sky dipped dangerously at the center; it gave the impression of a water-filled canvas. A distant muted rumble came from it, as though the canvas had begun to tear. Jim turned his head and stared blankly at me from the front door. "No answer," he said. He walked along the side of the house and disappeared around a corner.

I stayed where I was, watching the sky and the earth. A green chameleon slithered past my foot, its body turning dull brown as it crawled along a branch that had fallen in the rain, then changing back to green as it jumped off and went running into the wet grass. The cloud bank above the southern horizon had taken on a sickly yellowish tint. It was an eerie light for 11 o'clock in the morning. Except for the water that dripped from the leaves of the big oak and the gutter of the house, there was no sound. It was as quiet here as it had been in the center of the swamp. A window went up in the second story of the house and Jim stuck his head out. "Nobody's home," he said. "I climbed up the grape arbor. Attic window was open. Come on." His head disappeared, and after a moment the front door swung back. I followed him in. Jim

*A familiar sight in the fickle skies of southern Louisiana, storm clouds menace a willow-lined channel of the Atchafalaya River.*

made some joke about breaking into his own uncle's property, and we both pretended not to know that the house had been evacuated because of the coming storm.

The silence within the walls was as solid and tomblike as the silence outside. Except for the occasional cry of a bird, the world around us seemed to have died. By now we both wanted to leave, but neither of us had the guts to suggest running. I said something flip about getting out of the swamp before the swamp got us. "Where would we go?" Jim said. "Might as well sit it out here. Big enough house. . . ." He walked away before I could answer and opened the doors that gave onto a screened gallery outside.

The south side of the house faced a bayou that led into the swamp beyond; we stood on the gallery looking at the view. A grizzled swamp rabbit with bristling ears squatted on the near bank of the bayou, looking at us. Then it turned slowly and faced the southern bank. The sky in the south had turned a deeper yellow. We stood there without speaking. Jim heard the sound before I did. "Listen to them," he said. "Lord . . . listen to them."

He opened the screen door quickly and I went out after him. We stood on the grass between the house and the bayou. Then I heard the sound too. It seemed to be coming from the branches themselves, as if the swamp trees were calling out. "What is it?" I asked. "Herons," Jim said. "And blackbirds. And ibises probably, and warblers . . . all the swamp birds together."

We waited, listening to the eerie sound. It was unmistakable: the bird calls had changed. These were not mating cries, or flight notes such as those heard from a flock of geese on the wing. Instead the birds were calling all at the same time, many species at once, producing a sharp edgy sound like a wail. There was an ugliness in the collective noise, comparable to a human voice wavering on the edge of hysteria. As a child I had heard stories of the change in the sound of bird cries before a hurricane strikes, but I had never really believed them. I had not yet learned that some bayou-country legends are based in fact, and this was one of them.

An hour passed, I think, or two—my sense of time was lost. By now the noise of the birds had broken into its separate parts, gathered again into a single chorus, shattered once more, and ended. The quiet was back, and beyond the line of trees something flopped and splashed in the bayou. The grass glistened hard under a jaundiced sky. I don't know how long we stood there before the yellow turned abruptly into the color of copper. Then the wind started.

At first it did not seem bad. It came in from the east; leaves fluttered, and the grass bent. Then the light deepened, and the wind left as quickly as it had come. Jim nudged me hard and pointed excitedly. A cougar was slinking along the high limb of a tupelo gum, its body gleaming like a bar of gold caught in the copper glow of the sky. It leaped to the branch of another tree, and from there to the earth, the slow majestic arcs of its movements magnified in the humid air. For an instant after touching ground it froze, motionless; then it was gone. We did not see it bound off into the underbrush or slink behind a tree; it merely vanished from sight. Cougars are rare in the swamp; I had never seen one before, I have never seen one since. The last image of it remained like a brand on the retina, and I stood staring at space for a long time. I could still see the hot gold shape of the cat that was no longer there, when the wind came back.

The second gust was longer, but not much harder than the first; the interval after it was shorter. The third gust brought the rain. I started to go inside, but Jim grabbed my arm; he wanted us to wait and watch the storm as long as we could from outside. I had read enough to know that high winds, accompanied by heavy rains, usher in the most dangerous period of a hurricane, and I wasn't as entranced as Jim was by the prospect of the beauty of the coming storm. I was more inclined to see what could be done about making the house safer than it looked. Evidently Jim's uncle had left hurriedly when the storm changed its course; no storm shutters were up and only two windows had been taped. For a while we stayed outside watching, as time after time the trees across the bayou bent, seeming almost to double over. Moss bounced in the branches. Small objects and bits of things began to blow over the water, as twigs, leaves, pieces of bark and birds' nests broke loose.

Inside the house, I found a roll of tape on a window sill, and began to make an X across each pane of glass to prevent it from shattering. After a while Jim came in and helped me. His face looked flushed; his eyes glittered as if in fever. Many animals, humans included, work themselves up to a high pitch in the face of a hurricane; apparently, the body makes ready to protect itself with an extra dash of adrenaline. I wondered if the cougar that had vanished faster than my eye could follow had felt the same strange excitement. Jim and I worked silently, taping the panes of glass, listening to the wind rise. The tape ran out before we had finished with all the east windows on the ground floor of the house; we left the windows on the west unprotected. There was not much we could do about it. Jim went to the kitchen to check the food supply, and I went to latch the outer screen door, which was flapping loudly back and forth on the gallery. The gusts of wind were violent now. The rain fell, not with an even slant as it had before, but in fierce curls and streaks, hissing and lashing like whips of water through the trees. As I opened the inside door to get to the screen door, I saw a full-grown raccoon at the gallery railing staring at me. At first I thought it had huddled there to get out of the wind; then, from the angle of its head and the peculiar slant of its shoulders, I realized that its neck was broken. Probably it had crawled from the hackberry tree nearest the house to the roof and had been blown off trying to get to the gallery. Beyond the house the wind ripped savagely at the moss in the trees. Some moss came loose and streaks of gray flew over the grass like torn pieces of sky. I shut and latched both doors and went back to help Jim in the kitchen. "You were right," he said. "I guess it's coming to get us."

By now the wind was a fierce, endless shriek, rising and falling. Every so often something hit the roof or a side of the house, and the whole place seemed to shudder on its foundations. Through the kitchen window I saw a large, bulky dark object lumbering with difficulty against the wind, across the space between the gallery and the bayou. On its lee side, protected at least partially from the wind, was a much smaller but equally bulky-looking object. "Black bears," Jim said. We watched as the female and cub disappeared in the lashing streaks of water. The rain was so heavy we could no longer see the bayou, and the wind was coming stronger all the time.

The woods all around were being shaken, as if some giant invisible rage had unleashed itself on the bayou. Trees bent their branches wildly in every direction. A few small animals skittered across between them, too fast to be identified; leaves and vines twisted high in the air. Something struck the roof with a force that reverberated like an earthquake in the kitchen, and the lights went out. The wind screamed in the half-dark; debris began to collect on the outside of the windows, to be blown away and collect again in the next vicious gust. A burst and a loud shattering of glass from the living room told us that the tape had not worked for all of the east windows.

Then, with a violence that seemed methodical, the wind rose higher. Beyond the trees, the bayou was a shapeless dark mass of water with waves and whitecaps, and the mass was approaching the house. Already the near line of cypress and tupelo gum and hackberry were in water halfway up their trunks. The swamp seemed to be growing, feeding on the fury of the hurricane, threatening to whirl the house and everything it contained into the wilderness of air, water and land. Jim darted across the kitchen and looked outside at the truck. I could tell what he was thinking. "We couldn't make it," I said. He shrugged. "We'll try," he said, "if the water comes much closer."

We stood and watched as the churning lake that had once been a bayou came toward us through the trees. "If it reaches that hackberry," Jim said, looking at the tree trunk nearest the gallery, "we'll start." We kept our eyes on it, and 20 minutes later the water was lapping over its roots. "Let's go," Jim said. I found a rope in a cupboard and Jim tied it to his waist. I held one end so that I could anchor him and pull him back if necessary while he tried to make it to the truck. The noises were at their wildest now, first on one side of the house, then on the other; the scraping of swamp debris sounded as though the storm were clawing at the walls. Jim opened the front door and I tightened the rope behind him. Then through the lashes of rain I saw that there wasn't any point in his getting to the truck. The big oak in the yard had been snapped like a pencil; it was lying half on top of the truck, half behind it. In the deafening wind we had not even heard the tree fall. I pulled hard on the rope and Jim fought the wind to make it back the four feet he had walked. In those four feet I thought he might be going to die. The wind slammed him against the house, and the rope grew so taut I was afraid it would cut through him. But at last he got inside and shut and bolted the door—as if a door, or a bolt, could have any effect on a storm that might destroy the house as easily as the oak outside.

The kitchen and living room were ankle-deep in muddy water by now. We grabbed armfuls of canned goods from a shelf, along with a can opener, and ran upstairs. We sat in one of the bedrooms away from the windows and watched. There wasn't much else to do but wait and hope. Then, as if a giant cleaver had descended from the sky and cut off all sound, the wind stopped.

The rain no longer fell. Calm came so suddenly that neither of us knew what to make of it. For a moment we sat where we were, Jim on one twin bed, I on the other, staring into space. Then we jumped up and opened the windows.

Outside, the swamp, the entire wilderness, was as still and soundless as a vacuum. No trees, not even the moss, swayed. What had once been a bayou, and was now a lake surrounding the house, was speckled with drops falling from leaves and soaked branches. The air was heavier than ever and there was a choked feeling to it that made it difficult to breathe. "The eye," Jim said. "We must be in the eye."

We ran to the top of the stairs, then stopped. The water had come up to the third step. There was no point in trying to get out of the house any more—there was no way to leave and no place to go anyway. We went slowly to a window and looked out. The swamp was a glittering maze of broken branches, leaves and swollen water. The last drops shone like jewels in the scene of silent devastation. I remembered reading that especially along the coast the worst danger in the aftermath of a hurricane came from snakes that try to climb onto high ground or even the rafters of partly submerged houses to escape the encroaching water. We were already flooded, and the flood would get worse, and I wondered about the snakes.

Before that problem, we would have to face the second half of the storm. It would be at least as bad as the first, I knew. We sat on the window ledge and looked below us. In the rain gutter a pileated woodpecker lay smashed and dead, its body twisted, one wing bent double under it. The gutter itself had been torn loose; half of it stuck out from the eaves like a long broken bone. The silence was complete. We had been shouting in order to hear each other during the first part of the storm. Now the ticking of a bedside clock clucked out of the room behind us, sharp and loud, the only noise for miles around. It was marking the minutes until the eye passed and the far side of the hurricane struck.

We watched the wreckage in the wilderness and waited for the wind.

# The Spell of the Swampland

The storied bayous of literary tradition, those shadowy places of still water, Spanish moss and mystery, really do exist, and they are as numerous as the very different-looking bayous of Louisiana's hill country and of its marshes. Like those waterways, the poetic bayous have acquired their special character because of their particular setting—the swamps that cover vast areas of the south-central part of the state.

One such area is the Atchafalaya Basin, a great soggy expanse along the 150-mile course of the Atchafalaya River. Another is the sprawling region, about 60 miles northwest of New Orleans, where the Blind River and other streams interweave in a tangled skein. These low, flat swamplands are alluvial—built up and molded by river waters that have overflowed their natural levees and, through the millennia, have deposited an immeasurably huge cargo of particles of solid matter.

Regularly nourished by water and sediment, this alluvial soil is among the richest anywhere in the world. Vegetation in the swamps grows wildly, engulfing everything—and as it decays it further enriches the muck that nurtured it. The wealth of plant food attracts a variety of animals. Though none are exclusively swamp dwellers, they take easily to the environment. Many are aquatic, or at least amphibious, but deer and other land mammals also cope well with the watery surroundings.

The swamp bayou reflects its setting in all aspects. The prodigal vegetation encloses it in dim, leafy, vaulted chambers, an inner sanctum where the sun seems an intruder. The water of the bayou moves faintly and sluggishly, fluctuating in depth from time to time. Some of the water is pure and sweet, though often stained the color of dark tea by the bark and fallen leaves of trees growing in it. Some bayous are muddy and thick with sediment, others are covered from bank to bank with plants (right).

Both the swamp bayou and the terrain in which it lies represent yet another of the ambiguous compromises between earth and water that characterize much of the rest of Louisiana. Where there is solid land in the swamps, it often bears the mark of man—roads, houses and fishing shacks. But in the deeper reaches, where a boat is the only way to get around, a primeval world prevails, discovered yet inscrutable, accessible but supremely detached.

*A quiet stream, overhung with Spanish moss and carpeted with vegetation, exemplifies the classic swamp bayou. The lush green carpet on the water's surface, at first glance seen as scum or slime, is actually a delicate mosaic of the tiny leaves of duckweed, one of the world's smallest flowering plants.*

## A Splurge of Riotous Growth

Except for its dark waters, the element that most shapes the Louisiana swamp is its luxuriant vegetation, at once beautiful and ugly, airborne and earthbound, fragile and indestructible. Mosses, vines, trees, air plants, water plants, algae, ferns assault every surface, screening the bayous, disguising each contour and defining every vista.

Lord of all is the bald cypress, rising smooth-trunked and stately from the water, with its strange gnarled knees standing nearby like dwarf sentinels. The seeds of the cypress need water-saturated soil to germinate in, and the wood is extremely durable and resistant to rot, which makes the tree admirably suited to swamp conditions—and also makes it coveted for the construction of houses, picket fences and coffins.

Crowding the cypresses at water level are water hyacinths, which grow floating on the surface and spread irresistibly wherever there is water and enough sunlight. High above, the air plants, too, seize on anything that offers a foothold. They need no roots in the ground, getting nutrition from dust particles and the moist air, and they seek nothing from their host trees except support.

The air plants, or epiphytes, include tree orchids and resurrection fern, but unquestionably the foremost is Spanish moss. Not a moss at all, it hangs everywhere in poetic festoons, ethereal and haunting, the hallmark of the swamp.

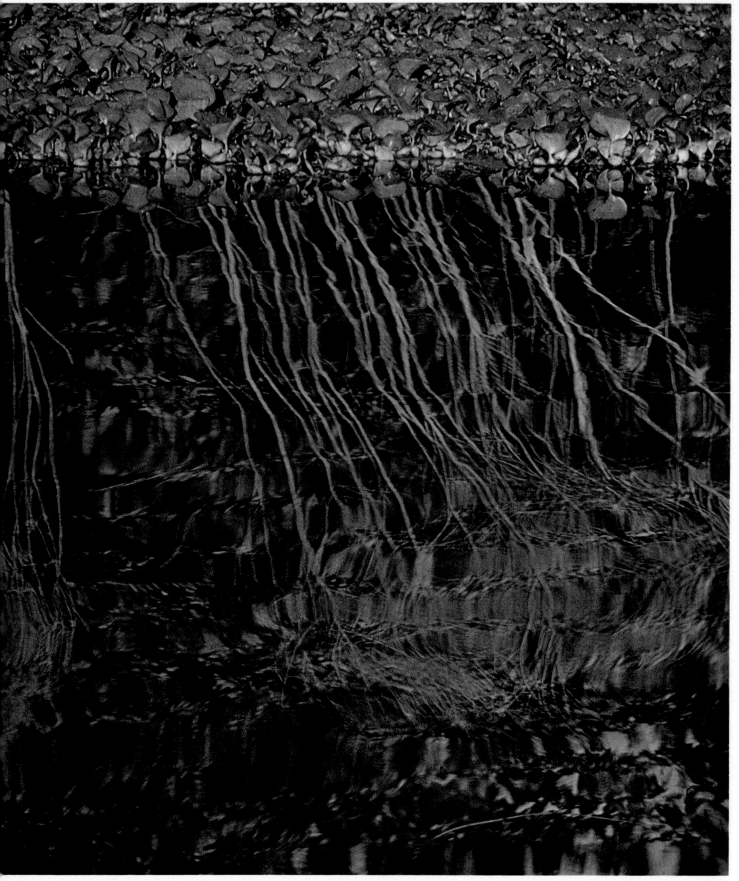

*Coffeeweed stems, rising from the bank beyond a bed of water hyacinths, are reflected upside down in the shimmering mirror of Blind River.*

Vines of Virginia creeper, fan-shaped palmetto leaves and green ash trees compete for space on the crowded bank of an Atchafalaya bayou.

Hardy butterweed adds yellow splashes to a layer of duckweed.

An aggressive water hyacinth displays a blossom of gentle hue.

Resurrection fern grows green again after turning brown in a dry spell.

Cypress knees, outgrowths of submerged roots, form a rampart for a pair of giants.

Spanish moss hangs thickly from the limbs and trunks

*of swamp trees, which it uses only for support. Tiny grayish scales on the surface of the stems give the ubiquitous air plant its ghostly color.*

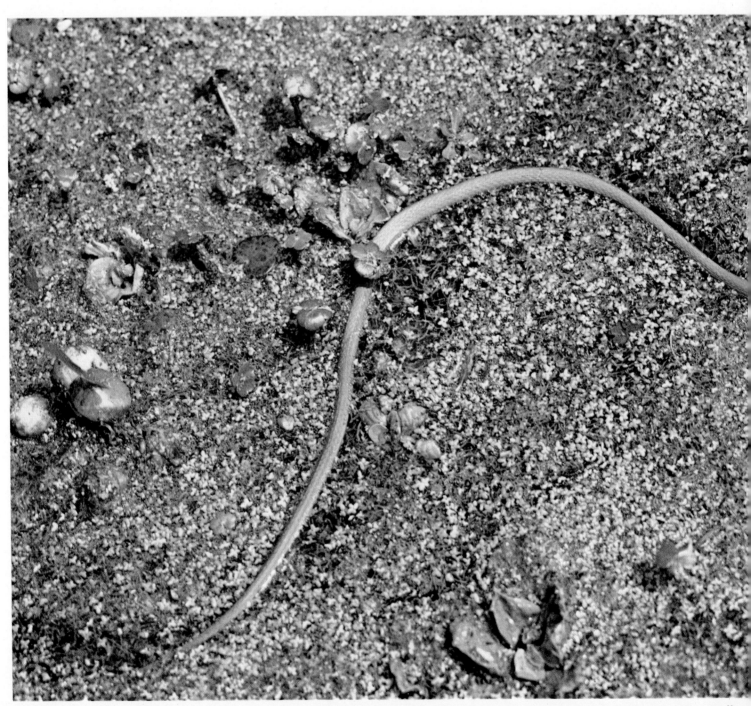

*A rough green snake swims lithely through a patch of pennywort and duckweed. One of the swamp's 15 nonvenomous species, it is actually*

## Creatures of Stealth and Silence

The animals of the swamp are sensed more than seen. Leaves quiver, a bush rustles, the bayou water ripples—the eye has to be quick to catch the signs, for they are quickly gone. Many creatures are exquisitely camouflaged, like the rough green snake at left, and blend superbly with their surroundings. Some spend most of their time partly submerged, like the alligator that lies with its dark, corrugated head just breaking the surface. Others are nocturnal and move silently under the protective cloak of darkness.

Reptiles, birds, mammals—all are in the swamp, each where it fits best. There are fewer birds than in the open marshes, but still ample numbers. The staccato *quock* of the stubby black-crowned night heron is a familiar echo in the swamp, and even the space-loving great egret comes to fish and sometimes nest there. Small mammals such as squirrels and swamp rabbits find haven where there is solid land. For the water lovers, of course, the places of shelter are almost limitless, and the bounty beyond compare. The shy otter and the gregarious raccoon feed on fish, crawfish and young amphibians; the raccoon's diet includes insects, small birds and plants as well.

Rarest of all mammals in the swamp are the bobcat and the black bear. Though they are almost never seen any more, the swamp affords them a last refuge against the pressures outside the wilderness.

*less at home in the water than in the trees, where it spends much of its time hunting insects.*

Its coat glistening, a rarely seen river otter suns on a safely isolated log.

A black-crowned night heron stalks a meal.

Baby raccoons, about two months old, cluster on a moldering tree stump.

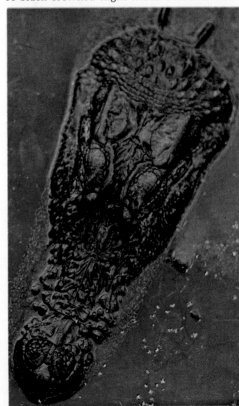

An alligator pokes its snout out of the water.

A white-whiskered nutria plows purposefully through a duckweed-spattered pond, alert to peril from its chief swamp predator, the alligator.

*A monarch butterfly, passing through the swamp during its springtime migration to the north, pauses among butterweed blossoms.*

# Flyers and Hoppers and Crawlers

Too small to dominate but too numerous to be overpowered, the insects of the swamp fill every possible niche with their trillions. Whatever the species, the insects are a basic food source for birds, fishes, reptiles, spiders and one another. Every year, for instance, hordes of mosquitoes provide a spring feast for dragonflies, which in turn make meals for birds and frogs; midsummer swarms of young lubber grasshoppers are good eating for everything from egrets to alligators.

In their turn, the insects act as scavengers, feeding on dead animals and on vegetation that would otherwise choke the swamp. Among the most assiduous are the fierce fire ants, whose colonies go at their task with a purposefulness that brooks no barrier (overleaf).

The ants and most other insects are permanent swamp dwellers; but the black and orange monarch butterfly is a visitor. One of the few types of butterflies that migrate, the monarchs travel to tropic regions in great swarms in autumn; on their way back north in spring they return as individual travelers, alighting here and there in the swamp.

Not actually insects, but heavily dependent on them for food, are the swamp's many kinds of spiders. One of the more extraordinary is the fishing spider, which makes the most of its environment through a knack for walking on water and eating small fish as well as insects.

*A fishing spider, which kills its prey with poison injections, lurks on a water-lettuce leaf.*

*A lubber grasshopper, grown to a formidable two and a half inches, rests between leaps.*

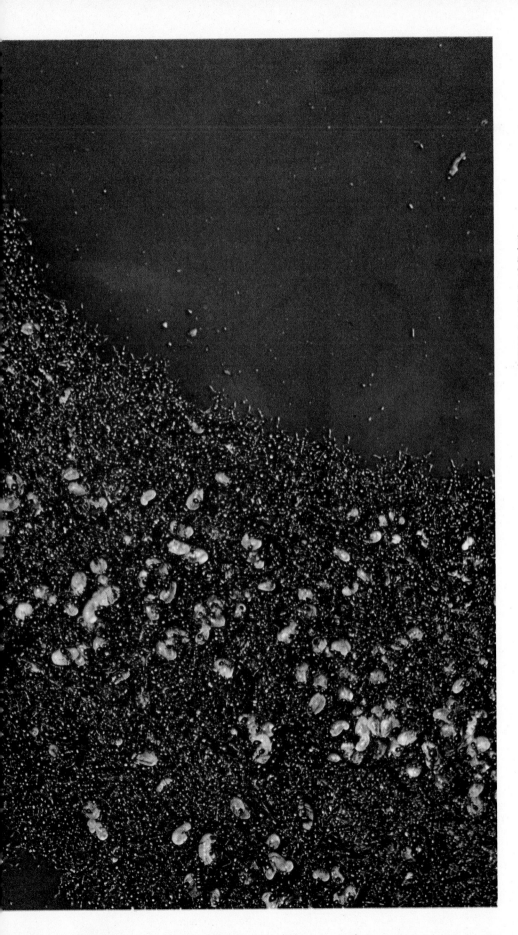

A column of fire ants, flooded out by
high water, crosses the surface of a
shallow bayou in search of dry land.
Though they are not aquatic, the ants
are so light that their mass does
not break the water's surface tension.
Those tightly packed in the center
carry the white pupal cases of their
young while the whole formation is
moved along by the current or a breeze.

As an early-morning autumn mist creeps over a cypress swamp in the Atchafalaya Basin, a solitary great egret waits on a log. Immobile, it

watches for an underwater movement or surface splash that will betray the whereabouts of its next meal—a young bluegill sunfish, perhaps.

# 4/ Violence and Aftermath

*Over their heads the towering and tenebrous boughs of the cypress/ Met in a dusky arch, and trailing mosses in mid-air/ Waved like banners that hang on the walls of ancient cathedrals.*    HENRY WADSWORTH LONGFELLOW/ EVANGELINE

There is no clearer way to understand the special nature of the struggle for survival in the bayou country than to see the area, and its inhabitants, under some form of stress. Jim and I began to understand it all too well as we waited for the second half of the hurricane to strike. We knew it must come and the animals seemed to know, or sense, it too. Amid the devastation, nothing moved. In the airless eye of the storm we waited, silent, like the swamp around us.

The house in which we had sought refuge stood surrounded by a boundless lake strewn with pieces of bark, branches, leaves, moss and the trunks of fallen trees. As we watched, a red maple that rose tall and strong 50 yards from the house appeared to stir. It shuddered in its leaves, was still, shook again, and began very slowly to dip to one side. With a sound like a grunt it toppled, disappeared beneath the water, then surfaced to float with the rest of the debris left by the storm. A young otter swam frantically out of its sunken branches. We stared at the dead maple. In the wake of the first terrific winds, its roots torn from its trunk, it had stood for several minutes as though still alive, like a soldier who has been shot but does not immediately fall. The lifeless tree seemed a bad omen in the gleaming yellow of the windless sky. Drops of water glittered over everything in sight. No animal ventured into the open; instinctively none trusted this long silence. The swamp stretched out, poised and rigid.

The winds came back as abruptly as they had left. We stationed ourselves near the inside wall of the big upstairs bedroom, facing away
from its windows. Through the windows of the smaller bedroom across
the hall we could see into the claw of the storm. The first half of the hurricane had come from the east. Now, from the west, the whips and lashes of air and water resumed. With an audible shiver the swamp began
again to twist under a slashing sky. Branches and broken roof shingles
scraped and bounced above us. An explosion from below announced
the cave-in of another wall of windows on the first floor.

Twice an animal of some kind clattered over the house, its screeches
cut short as the wind took its life. The first sound was the wailing of a
cat—a cougar, perhaps, or a bobcat. The second was louder and more
shrill, and whatever was making it struck the chimney with a hard dull
blow. A flutter of something large, white and feathery streaked down
past the far windows. "Egret," Jim said. "It's funny—they almost never
get caught—not in the open sky." Then, staring through the windows,
he added, "There is no sky."

Through the sheets of rain that blew against the glass, the view outside was distorted and mangled, as if the heart of the swamp had burst
from the force of the pressure above it. The moss in some of the cypress trees pointed straight up. A lash of gray slapped the house, and in
the far bedroom two panes seemed at first to tremble, to stretch, then
to melt into the room. Slivers of glass shone for an instant in a long
spurt of water. Then thin rivulets rolled across the floor toward us, driv-
en through the empty squares that had been the panes. The house had
started to disintegrate into the moaning wind, which seemed to be in
mourning for itself.

Suddenly, when it seemed that the house could not hold out much
longer, the walls shuddered—like the maple tree in the instant before it
fell—and just as abruptly the moaning ceased. But the wind began
again, resurged to buffet the west side of the house in a last lethal
burst, fluttered, and left. The rain continued to fall, but almost list-
lessly now, a wet shroud hanging from the sky, swinging back and
forth above a swamp that had been turned into an open grave.

Ten minutes later we ventured out of the room to the top of the
stairs. But even as I started down, Jim grabbed my arm and pulled me
back. The level of swamp water on the first floor had risen nearly a
fourth of the way up the staircase. Stretched across the last visible step
was a trio of snakes, each about three feet long, with triangular black-
ish heads. Cottonmouths. One of the creatures opened its mouth,

revealing a pinkish-white inner membrane that did indeed look like cotton. "We may have to wait quite awhile," Jim said.

He went back to the bedroom and I stood staring at the snakes. It was not the first time I had seen cottonmouths, for they are common in the bayou country, the most numerous of the six poisonous species of snakes found in Louisiana. Now, however, I could not stifle the wild hope that these invaders were not cottonmouths after all, that they belonged to one of the 33 harmless species to be found in the state. I studied them carefully as they lolled on the stairs below.

Each had about a dozen dark, wide crossbands, olive brown in color. The underside of the tail and the rear of the belly were black. I could see the loreal pits just below and in front of the eyes, and the vertically elliptical pupils. Clearly the snakes were cottonmouths, dealers in a poison for which Jim and I had no antidote anywhere within miles—crucial hours away.

The snakes appeared to be on the stairs to stay. And even if we could get past them, their presence inside the house promised that there would be many more snakes in the water outside—a formidable obstacle between us and the nearest dry land. Swimming through the flood would not help; snakes can and do bite underwater.

Snakes! Both Jim and I were wearing boots of a soft leather that could easily be pierced by their fangs, the elongated hollow teeth through which the venom is discharged to kill prey. Fangs grow in pairs, one on each side of the mouth, and there are usually several smaller sets in reserve, moving frontward as they grow. To ensure the sharpness of its bite, a snake changes fangs every two or three weeks; as the front fangs grow blunt or break off, the set behind them will move into position.

People unaware of the phenomenon have sometimes discovered it the hard way. Sometimes a bayou visitor traps a baby snake and removes the fangs—with the prudent use of pliers held in gloved hands —intending to raise a harmless and unique pet. The pet, of course, turns out to be anything but harmless.

Jim came back with a half-consumed can of beans and I spooned it up, my eyes still fixed on the stairs. One of the snakes had moved a step higher. I remarked that the water was rising, too. Jim nodded. "Won't come up much farther," he said, "but it won't need to."

I followed him to the bedroom windows and looked out. A vast drowned world lay around us. I had heard about the deluge of salt-water waves that accompany hurricanes in coastal areas. But a flood

*A highly unusual sight in the bayous or anywhere else, a hanging honeybees' nest is suspended from a branch in the Atchafalaya swamp. Honeybees usually build their combs in the crotch of a tree or in a hollow of the trunk; this colony was probably forced to relocate to emergency quarters by a natural disaster that ruined the original nest.*

caused only by wind and rain was something I had neither seen nor heard about, short of the Old Testament.

There was still some wind, as if an afterthought of the hurricane. A shrub went bobbing past the house. It was a buttonbush, common in the swamp, its dark green leaves gleaming around the little balls of white that give the plant its name. It seemed alive, bouncing gaily along in the flood. As it dipped behind a partly submerged cypress trunk, something else caught my eye. What appeared to be a mound of black earth was drifting, heavily and slowly, on the far side of the trunk; I could not make out what it was until I saw a small black bear cub, perched above it on the trunk. The cub descended, tentatively prodded the body of its mother with one paw, then climbed back about a third of the way up the tree waiting for her to respond. "It'll leave her," Jim said, "when it gets hungry enough." Some time later we noticed that the cub had at last deserted the corpse of its mother and gone off foraging through the water for food.

The night came, soundless; even the frogs were quiet now. Jim and I sprawled on the twin beds of the big bedroom. We dozed fitfully. At moments one or the other of us would get up and move restlessly about, prowling the second floor of the house and trying to remember to avoid the stairs. With the morning the sky, cloudless and crystalline blue, gleamed brighter than I had ever seen it, as if the storm had polished the arch of blue above us as sand polishes stone. The Spanish moss hung straight and still in the trees, over a flood that had lowered somewhat overnight. Here and there the water's glassy surface was broken by surreptitious movements, too tentative to be identifiable but unmistakably the work of living things. From between two tupelo-gum trees came the dark brown furry back of a nutria, swimming determinedly northeast; the animal seemed to know where it was going. A plop in the water just ahead of the nutrias signaled a fish jumping.

As we sat on a window sill surveying the scene, Jim jumped up, frowning. "I'm going to have another look inside that chest," he said. During the night, he had gone rummaging through every box and drawer in both bedrooms and in the attic, looking for anything that might prove useful to us in getting away from the flood. Now he ducked into the attic and emerged a minute later carrying a pair of torn but heavy hip boots. Jim had rejected them during his first search because the soles flapped and water would seep in through them. "Water doesn't matter," he explained, "if I can get as far as the garage without being bitten by anything. There ought to be a rowboat. Everybody who owns a house around here keeps a skiff of some kind."

He took a broom from the hall closet and went to the top of the stairs. Two of the cottonmouths had gone during the night, but one was still there. One poisonous snake was just as bad as three, as far as I was concerned; but Jim took a metal book end from the small bedroom and aimed it down the staircase. It struck four or five steps above the snake and bounced down loudly. The snake slithered off into the water. Jim started down, moving the broom in a wide arc ahead of him, sweeping and stirring the surface of the water. When he reached the bottom step, the muddy water was well over his knees, about two inches short of the top of the hip boots. "I think I can make it," he said, and slogged out the door. I ran back to the window and watched him heave through the water toward the garage, still swinging the broom. Once he flipped something out of his path. "Snapping turtle," he called. "The water here's like thin mud . . . feels as if the earth's melted."

Half an hour later we were both sitting in the small skiff he had found in the garage. He had poled the boat over to the door of the house, as near to the stairs as he had been able to manage, and I had half-slid, half-flown down the stairs to join him, sopping wet but unmolested by snakes. I began to row as Jim fiddled with an outboard motor that refused, of course, to function. Around and above us, the vines of trumpet creepers dangled, torn loose from the branches. A few of their orange blossoms had survived—flashes of color in the moss. We passed the body of an opossum floating belly down. I turned it over with an oar. It was clinging to a branch as though, even in death, it felt safer that way.

Two water snakes crisscrossed ahead of the boat, and beyond them a big bullfrog jumped from a rise of earth onto a torn lily pad that had no stem and was too soft to hold the frog's weight. It tried to jump back, but the pad sank so quickly that it was forced to swim. I watched as it made its way back to the rise of earth, moving heedlessly past one of the snakes. The bullfrog's careless disregard of its traditional predator was curious.

Then I noticed something even more curious. Two other animals were waiting on the rise for the flood to ebb. A bobcat and a large swamp rabbit were sitting only a few feet apart, as unconcerned by each other's presence as the frog had been of the snake. The frog positioned itself between the bobcat and rabbit, and all three creatures stared fixedly at the flood. As we drifted past, not one of them took any notice of us.

*A company of brown pelicans drifts lazily along a coastal waterway after feeding. The state bird of Louisiana, and once as common there as cypress and the water hyacinth, the pelican is now an endangered species, seriously threatened by heavy pesticide concentrations in the fish it eats.*

In the immediate wake of a flood, a kind of truce may prevail among the shocked animals. For a few hours, for a day and a night, enemies are not enemies; there is a pause in the killing. Then, as the shock wears off, hunting resumes, with more risk than ever to the small creatures that have been dislocated by the floodwaters and can no longer escape into the safety of a familiar burrow or tree. Exhausted by the ordeal of the storm, wood rats, squirrels, opossums, even birds become such easy prey that their populations—already diminished by the hurricane—are further reduced.

Our skiff drifted from shoal to shoal, touching a sunken log here, ricocheting gently off the top of a cypress knee there. Jim had given up trying to fix the motor. He pointed over my shoulder. I turned in time to see a white-tailed deer, a full-grown buck, on a rise in the distance. He was rubbing his antlers against a tree trunk. The antlers, which had started growing in February or March after the old set was shed, were fully developed by now, some six months later, and the skinlike "velvet" that covered the tines was beginning to dry up and peel off. As the velvet shrivels, it makes the antlers itch so that what looks like a polishing operation is actually a way for the deer to scratch himself.

We rowed around for hours near the house in a kind of trance, letting the boat drift when an occasional current took it, feeling our way in an uncertain world that glistened freshly. Life was reaching up through the flood. The reaction to the effort for survival imbued each plant or animal with a surge of energy that was almost visible. The clear blue sky provided a brilliant backdrop to the scene that remained untarnished throughout the day. In the humid stillness a great bubble of sunlight capped the earth like a natural hothouse, and all living things stretched open inside it. By midafternoon the swamp was in motion. It crept and tingled around our skiff, oddly sensual in its reaffirmation of life. The surrounding wetness acted like a magnifying glass. Each cypress leaf or streamer of moss looked larger than before. Each edge of a plant, each color, stood out—etched, vivid. Jim said, "It's like being inside a diamond."

It was late afternoon before we remembered that our purpose in taking the skiff had been to leave the flooded area. Our families would be worried; we knew we ought to contact them by nightfall. We rowed past the flooded house in the direction of the road we had driven on to get there. At last patches of dry land appeared ahead. When the water under us was shallow enough, Jim stepped out and grounded the skiff. I got out after him and we moved slowly, single file, through the slosh, each of us carrying an oar that we had taken along as a precautionary weapon. Jim, moving ahead of me, spotted a cottonmouth on a log; reflexively, he lunged at it with his oar. The snake struck his leg almost lazily, fastening its fangs in his right boot; they did not, however, pierce through the rubber. Jim yelled at me to get around to his other side; he remembered not to reach down with his hands, and the snake slid off the boot and curved away into the water.

As we walked on, I thought about Jim's reckless attack on the snake, odd behavior for someone so knowledgeable about swamp creatures. In time, I was to realize that Jim had been in a state approaching euphoria. Just as men and animals become more alert in an emergency, so the letdown afterward and the promise of escape can have the opposite effect; behavior grows careless. In the end it was luck more than anything else that got us out of the flooded area soon after sundown. With the disappearance of the light, the truce among the animals seemed to end. From the edge of the swamp, in the darkness, we could hear far-off cries, and directly above us a screech owl shrieked.

During the weeks that followed, I found myself needing to return to the place Jim and I had seen during the hurricane—as though my sense of the world would remain incomplete until I saw the swamp with its balance returned. In the fall I drove back. This time I went alone. From the bank where the house stood, the bayou appeared peaceful and quiet. Jim's uncle had been at work on his battered property. He had boarded over the windows he had not had time to reglaze, and the fallen oak and the old truck crushed by it had been cleared away.

The woods around the house were strewn with branches and vines, brought low where they would provide forage for the swamp rabbits and deer. The hurricane had not taken a significant toll of the swamp rabbits, I knew; even when only half-grown, they swim well enough to reach floating pieces of wood and ride out the storm. New litters would quickly compensate for the young that had drowned.

Deer, needing sturdier supports for use as rafts, probably had not fared so well. In the long run, though, the deer population would benefit from the blowdown of succulent tree tips, mistletoe, greenbrier and poison ivy. Where high winds had leveled acres of timber, underbrush would soon sprout in profusion to provide future generations of deer with both food and fawning cover.

Here and there beside the bayou a whole tree lay rotting, already a host to the mushrooms that deer relish. Scattered along the banks of the stream were dead fish. Some had been tossed up in the hurricane itself. Others had died a slower death later, as leaves accumulating and decaying in the water used up the oxygen. Except for a few gray squirrels twittering near the grape arbor, I noticed no other animal survivors.

Even the squirrels might disappear from the place if they ran out of food. The hurricane had whipped away much of the trees' seed crop —the acorns, hackberries and pecans on which the squirrels depended. I had heard tales of the migrations of gray squirrels: hundreds of them, of all ages, moving through woods and swimming across waters in a mass exodus from a territory where their population had outrun the local food supply.

The orphan bear cub was nowhere to be seen. Most animals of the swamp, including the black bear, are secretive nocturnal creatures, and only special or dire circumstances, such as a hurricane, will drive them into the open during daylight hours. The cub, the bobcat and the cougar that Jim and I had seen in August could have been holed up somewhere not too far away, sleeping by day to hunt by night, or they could have moved on to a less-damaged part of the swamp. Bears can survive as vegetarians if they have to; but wildcats must have meat, so that when a hurricane kills the small animals and birds on which they feed, they often leave for another territory, making their exodus singly rather than in hordes the way squirrels do.

There was loneliness in the swamp now. I left quickly and drove several miles to where a patch of pine trees spread their shade across a sandy slope. I took a book and a blanket and stretched out to read. It was one of those gentle, humid days that make the earth feel safe, and it was hard to remember that the ugly violence of a hurricane had passed here so recently. I dozed for a while, then woke and lay still, looking for animals in the trees above my head. I saw none.

But, on the earth next to me, something coral red glinted and moved. I turned my head slowly, hoping that the thing beside me would not notice the movement. The muscles in my neck cramped from the effort. Finally, my face lay at an angle that allowed me to see the coral-red object. It took what seemed an age before I understood what it was that I was looking at.

First I thought that it must be a flower. Then I saw that it was not a flower but the circular base of a plant, no bigger than an inch across, from which rose a single, thin stem. It was the base itself that was coral colored, shaped like a starfish with many legs; each ended in a

*Balanced on its spindly perch, a Louisiana heron looks all neck, wings and legs. But when fishing in its native marsh it is, like other wading birds, extremely efficient. It stands in the water, extends its wings and pirouettes, casting a shadow that both attracts its aquatic prey and cuts down surface glare to make the prey more visible; the heron's long neck and bill are well designed for snaring the catch with a quick darting thrust.*

round pod covered with hundreds of minute tentacles that appeared to be in motion. At the tip of each tentacle was a single drop of a glittery, sticky-looking substance that gave the whole base the look of a meticulously fashioned jewel. Caught in one of the pods was an ant; it was raising its legs one by one in a frantic effort to release itself from the crystal drop of mucilage. As it struggled, the drops of moisture grew larger. The pod in which the insect was by now hopelessly stuck began very slowly to close. Tentacles from below and outside the pod curved upward until the ant was buried inside.

I sat up fast and looked around. There were about 20 more of the plants—sundews, they are called—behind the one next to me. Two were closed; the others lay open, their delicate coral tentacles spread out, waiting to trap, devour and digest any insect that came along. Twice more insects lighted on the surface of the plant pods, only to be caught in one of the drops of liquid.

There are 90 varieties of sundews around the world, all of them worth watching. After a while, I took a key from my pocket and touched one of the pods. Nothing happened. I prodded it—still nothing happened. The syrupy drops at the tips of the tentacles did not increase, nor did the plant stir. It was not until much later, when I came across something Charles Darwin had written, that I understood why. In 1875, reporting on his own observations of sundews, Darwin said: "After feeding the leaf pods [with] insects, beginning actions of digestion took place. Then on other leaf pods sand, then glass, then artificial insects were placed; however, the plant would not react to the foreign matter. The plant knows! It appears to sense that these materials are not food it can utilize. The leaves won't curl, the tentacles do not react, and no juices form. Amazing!"

The bayou country provides a hospitable home for the sundew, as well as for another insect eater: the pitcher plant. Both grow in acid bogs or sandy places whose soil does not provide enough nutrients—nitrate and phosphate in particular—to support most other plants. The pitcher plant, which hybridizes so often that it is seldom easy to differentiate among its nine species, is no less amazing than the sundew, and has a splendid diversity of colors. The most common are the purple and the crimson pitcher plants. The purple variety has a flower of reddish purple, thinning to an orange or rose color the nearer to the Louisiana coast the plant grows; its leaves are mottled yellows and reds. The crimson pitcher plant has bright red flowers, about three inches across, with leaves veined in red and white. Added to the flamboyance of color is the remarkable shape the leaves take. As they grow—as much as two feet in the case of the crimson variety, no higher than eight inches in the purple variety—the leaves curl together to form a cone, much like a trumpet in shape, closed at the bottom and flaring open and wide at the top. The cone serves as a receptacle for rain water, a fact that led the early Spaniards in Louisiana to liken the plant to a pitcher—the name it has borne ever since.

The pitcher plant not only holds water, but secretes a sweet liquid inside its cone that attracts insects. Unlike the "active" sundew, the "passive" pitcher plant does not move to capture its prey. When a beetle or an even larger insect starts down inside the cone, it encounters partway a lining of infinitesimal white hairs, as slippery as they are invisible. No longer able to sustain a foothold, the insect slides toward the liquid at the bottom of the cone. Even if it is able to stop its fall, it cannot climb back up, for the hairs all point downward to form a barrier. Sooner or later the insect will plunge into the liquid, drown, decompose and be digested. Its skeleton remains stored deep inside the cone. A different ending awaits the insect devoured by the sundew. Its skeleton is released by the plant to be blown away on the first passing breeze.

For hours that afternoon I watched the sundews. Growing on relatively high ground, safe from flood, they were among the tiniest survivors of the summer's disaster. The most delicate-looking life in the bayou country often proves to be the sturdiest.

I caught another glimpse of bayou life during that solitary outing. As dusk approached, I spotted a raccoon rummaging for food in a shallow stream. Raccoons, as even suburban dwellers know, will eat anything they find on land, including the garbage at the back door. But here in the watery wilderness the raccoon is the consummate fisherman, expertly scooping up fish, frogs, crawfish and salamanders with its slender-fingered paws. So ingrained is its association of water with food that a captive raccoon may wet even a sugar lump before eating it. For years zoologists attributed such acts simply to the raccoon's desire to wash its food, and indeed the scientific name for the raccoon is *Procyon lotor*—*lotor* being Latin for "one who washes." But more recently the raccoon's behavior has been recognized as merely a way of recreating the conditions under which it naturally finds food.

As I watched the raccoon deftly fishing for its supper, I thought of the other common nocturnal hunter of the bayou country, the opossum. The contrast between the two is interesting. The raccoon's

*Beyond an array of cypress knees, a toppled bald cypress lies and rots—victim of a violent storm that shook the Atchafalaya swamp.*

wiliness is legendary; it can outsmart a pack of the best-trained hound dogs. The opossum, on the other hand, puts on a show that deceives no hunter. It does not try to run when cornered, but feigns death—"plays possum." It falls limp, clamps its eyes shut, lolls its tongue; even its heartbeat slows down. But what it may lack in persuasiveness it makes up for in fertility. There can be as many as 18 babies to a litter, and two or even three litters a year. Possums are marsupials—relatives of the kangaroo. They are born underdeveloped, about the size of bees, and —like baby kangaroos—they spend their first month or two inside their mother's pouch, clinging to her nipples. Often, during this period some of them perish for want of nourishment; a female possum has 11 or 13 nipples, and if she has produced a large litter the demand for her milk outruns the supply. The survivors venture from the pouch when they reach the size of mice; for a while, until they can manage on their own, they have a distinctive mode of getting about—traveling on their mother's back, their toes clinging to her fur.

I was tempted to stay in the pine grove studying the raccoon at the stream and hoping that a possum—or perhaps a bear—might appear. But as the light faded, prudence prevailed. I got into my car and drove back to the bustle of the city.

A few months later, in early winter, I went back to see how the wild creatures of the Atchafalaya had recovered from the ravages of the August hurricane. This time I was on the west bank of the river, where the swamp begins. I had been hiking for more than an hour and had paused to rest when I saw a white-tailed buck, the points of his antlers glistening. This was mating season—a period that lasts in Louisiana from early December into late January.

White-tailed deer are polygamous; several bucks frequently stalk the same doe. When rivals meet, a battle follows with each buck using his antlers to shove the other away from the doe, to gore his rival or throw him to the ground. The antlers are defensive tools as well; although the tines may be as sharp as those of pitchforks, they are arranged in a basket shape that serves to ward off blows. Actually, the worst peril for the rival bucks is the possibility that their antlers will become firmly interlocked; then both deer starve to death. As long as the rut—the period of sexual excitement—lasts, each buck prowls alone, staying with one doe for just a few days before running off to look, and fight, for another. Only afterward do herds of males and females congregate peaceably again.

I sat motionless and watched as the buck moved from tree to tree. In his winter coat of thick gray hair—in the blue, hunters call it—he was camouflaged, quite difficult to see against the background of dark tree trunks. Then, without thinking, I lifted my hand to scratch my knee. The buck stiffened, bent his head, lowered his upraised tail so that it no longer showed the "white flag" of fur on the underside—and melted into the underbrush. For a long time I sat waiting; the buck did not come back. When the day waned and the sun turned red through the cypress leaves, I decided to leave. But first I took off my belt and tied it to a branch of the tree under which I had been sitting, to mark the place.

Early the following autumn I went back to the west bank of the Atchafalaya River. After more than a day of searching, I found the tree with my belt still tied to it. I sat down again to wait. No buck appeared. But as the afternoon progressed I saw a doe behind the trees, poised and delicate, incredibly elegant, followed by a small fawn. The doe still wore her lightweight reddish summer coat; the fawn was nearly three months old and beginning to lose its white polka dots. Her first fawn, I thought. Except for the first birth, a doe usually bears twins. Heedless of my presence, the doe and the fawn went on eating greenbrier from a patch behind the tree line, and I kept my eyes on them until they disappeared, still browsing.

A heavy plop in the river and a flutter in the branches overhead reinforced the message that creatures were thriving underwater and in the sky as well as on the land. The air and the water cling to the earth in this place—each separate, yet each part of the whole—each a matrix of life in some form. Another spring, another summer, had come and gone. The bayou country lay calm and gentle, the hurricane of the previous year now a distant memory.

# The Hospitable Marsh

As the land of Louisiana stretches south toward the Gulf of Mexico, the dark swamp bayous of towering cypresses and dangling Spanish moss give way to a vast and virtually treeless area of marshes stippled with ponds and coarse grasses. From afar these wetlands, flat and open to the sky, appear monotonously unchanging. Nothing much seems to be going on except for the rhythmic swaying of grasses moved by the wind blowing off the Gulf.

The appearance is deceptive. The nearly five million acres of marshland bordering Louisiana's coast, extending inland from 10 to 60 miles, sustain an intense year-round concentration of plant and animal life. Blessed with bright sunshine, thick black soil and protected brackish waters, the marshes provide as extensive a nursery and haven for fish, crustaceans and water birds as can be found anywhere on the continent. More than 100 species of fishes either spawn or live in the marshes. Nearly a third of all North America's species of birds are either permanent or winter residents; birds whose breeding habitats are a continent apart come together to feed in this hospitable place.

Differences become softened here, where land and earth are often indistinguishable and where fresh water and salt blend in a mix that changes with each tide or wind shift. Gulf fish are sometimes found miles up the marsh bayous; salt-water and fresh-water fish often swim side by side. Animals that are swimmers at one time become overland travelers at others; prominent among them are the marshland's 170,000 alligators. Crawfish in the millions spend their early days along the pond bottoms, but as adults they often come to the surface to feed.

Even the changing seasons reflect the state of gentle compromise that characterizes the marshland. Average temperatures vary from summer to winter less than almost anywhere else in the United States, and seasonal contrasts in the look of the land are muted. But changes do occur. Each of the seasons has its own rhythm, and the differences between winter and spring are particularly noticeable. The one resounds to the clamor of invading migratory waterfowl; the other hums with the activity of new generations of animals and plants. In the meantime, during the brief transition between the two seasons, the marshland enjoys a quiet period of respite (right).

*Serene in the evening light of late February, a Gulf Coast marsh bears the scars of a recent onslaught by winter visitors. The watery gaps in the foreground are "eat outs," areas where geese—abetted by muskrats—have torn up the three-cornered grass that is their favorite food. Eventually new plants will grow to close the gaps.*

## A Rip-Roaring Winter Resort

Winter in the marsh is a lively, noisy time filled with the whistling beat of strong wings and the raucous gabble of half a million blue geese and snow geese that have come south on their annual migration. Their arrival itself, wave upon wave over a period of about six weeks, is a sight to behold —and hear. The geese have traveled a long way, setting out as early as the end of September from their chill native tundra near the Arctic Circle, heading directly down the middle of North America, and touching down on the Louisiana coast about three or four weeks later.

The major influx over, the geese settle in, splashing about, honking and hunting for their preferred winter fare: three-cornered grass. Their powerful bills grub so voraciously at the fat roots of the plants that when they finish with an area there is no vegetation left at all.

By the first of March the blues and snows, rested, well fed and sleek, have started back north, mating en route, to lay their eggs and raise their young among rivulets of thawing ice in their Arctic barrens. In the Louisiana marshes, their strident cries are replaced by the delicate trills of the orchard oriole, common yellowthroat and other songbirds, which have come home for the summer after wintering in Central and South America. They join the year-round population of great egrets, bitterns and rails, and the cycle of teeming bird life begins anew.

*A flock of blue and snow geese reconnoiter a marsh in the Sabine Wildlife Refuge near*

the Gulf Coast, ready to swoop at the sight of a tempting stand of grass. They may travel as much as 70 miles in pursuit of a feed.

Blue and snow geese gobble grit from
the bottom of a sandy pond in the
Sabine refuge. Like most wild fowl,
geese need this substance for digestion.
They are toothless, and the grit, lodged
in their muscular gizzards, helps
grind up the food they cannot chew.

Two Canada geese—a new strain that
never goes to Canada but lives all year
in Louisiana—survey a pond in
the Rockefeller Wildlife Refuge. Some
150,000 of the original breed used to
winter here before Midwestern
grainfields lured many of them away.

*At winter's end, a blue goose and a snow goose take off from the marsh to join the flocks headed north. Members of the same species*

—differing only in color and markings—they travel about 4,500 air miles in the annual trek to and from their southern feeding grounds.

*A protectively colored least bittern, a full-time marsh resident, forages in new coco grass.*

*Lured from hibernation by a warm sun and rising waters, a cottonmouth prowls for food.*

## A Gentle Change to Spring

Spring comes subtly in the marshland, without the dramatic rebirth that follows a stark northern winter. Because of the equable winter temperatures of the subtropical Gulf Coast and a growing season that extends from early February to mid-December, the onset of spring is hard to pinpoint. It brings changes though, and many new beginnings.

A fresh crop of wild millet awaits nesting songbirds; cattails and three-cornered grass that the wintering birds depleted are being replenished to nourish newborn muskrats and nutria. Marsh grasses also provide a nursery for fish, shrimp, oysters and crabs just in from their birth in the Gulf, and furnish a protective cover for the newly laid eggs of insects, birds and alligators.

With new food and new life, the marsh becomes a stalking ground for the predator. The cottonmouth snake seeks the eggs or nestlings of birds like the red-winged blackbird and the least bittern. The birds, in turn, are on the alert for some tasty insect —a mosquito or a larger mouthful in the form of a damsel fly.

On occasion the steady rhythms of springtime are jarred by cataclysm as the Mississippi goes on a rampage so mighty its floodwaters reach all the way to the marshes. Many creatures of the marsh drown or are forced to flee, and great swaths of vegetation are swept away. But the waters always recede and the marsh always recovers.

A male red-winged blackbird, perched amid blooming rushes, conspicuously flaunts his red epaulets during the spring breeding season.

Waiting to snap up a passing insect,
this damsel fly clings motionless to a
blade of marsh grass. A delicate
kin of the dragonfly, it catches its
prey on the move, scooping it up in
midair with a quick, graceful dart.

Raised more than two feet above
normal by rainfall and wind tides, the
swollen water of a coastal marsh poses
a threat to vegetation, which it
may carry away, as well as to animals,
which it may either drown or drive
out. But the rich layer of new sediment
deposited by the disturbed, muddy
waters will benefit future generations
of marsh plants and creatures.

# 5/ The Underwater Forest

*. . . a properly protected marsh cannot be depleted.*
*It continually produces, like the legendary pitcher of wine*
*that is never emptied.*   WILLIAM A. NIERING/ *THE LIFE OF THE MARSH*

Where swamps and marshes meet in southern Louisiana, bayous become the trails of a vast underwater forest. Like a land forest, the aquatic kind is an environment all its own, with plants providing the basic foods as well as the protective cover for creatures large and small. As the waters run their southerly course, turning from fresh to brackish to salt as they mix with tides from the Gulf of Mexico, the denizens of this forest differ from zone to zone. But each area has its innumerable inhabitants, and just about anything that can crawl, hop, swim or plop is worth watching.

There is, for instance, the crawfish, also known as crayfish, crawdad, stone crab, mini-lobster or mud bug. Whatever it is called, the little armored beast abounds in Louisiana, and affords a fine excuse for spending some time in the wilder reaches of the southern bayou country. I remember one weekend long ago when my friend Jim and I went on a crawfish expedition in the lower Atchafalaya Basin. It was in March—the start of the four-month crawfish season—and what we had in mind was not studying the crawfish in its habitat, but catching and eating as many as we could.

Louisiana's brief winter had begun to turn into a wet spring, and as we drove southwest from New Orleans, on a dirt road pitted with clamshells and packed with dust, the daylight faded and trees alongside that had been bright and sparkling wet became ghostly and angular.

The road twisted and changed direction many times before we found a deserted spot beside a stream near the southernmost edge of the basin and pitched our tent. To the north of us, within the basin itself, the back waters of Belle River, Bayou Sorrel and Little Bayou Pigeon were and are famous for good crawfish catching, but it was a matter of pride for us to find our own secret place and make a big haul with enough left over to take home.

Jim and I considered ourselves experts on crawfish. The truth is that we knew only the more obvious facts—where to find them and how to cook and eat them. We did not know that there are at least 300 species in the world ranging from an inch to a foot long; or that there are more than 100 species in the United States; or that there are 29 in Louisiana, of which two—the red swamp crawfish and the white river crawfish —are the most common.

Like all animals, crawfish must consume oxygen and eliminate carbon dioxide to live. Like certain other crustaceans, crawfish can draw oxygen from the air, but derive their main supply from the oxygen molecules that are dissolved in the water and absorbed through their gills. The amount of dissolved oxygen in the underwater forest varies widely, depending on such matters as the flow rate of a stream (the faster it goes, the more oxygen it takes in); the temperature of the water (the cooler it is, the more oxygen it can hold); and the abundance of aquatic vegetation (the more plants, up to a certain point, the more oxygen they can contribute). The red swamp crawfish, which can get by on a low supply of dissolved oxygen, predominates in the southernmost bayous, while the white river crawfish, which needs more oxygen, is more prevalent in the northern part of the state, where streams are better aerated.

Cheerfully unaware of all this science, convinced simply by a feeling that we were going to find the best place for red crawfish, we slept soundly under the branches of a hackberry tree. I woke to the smell of catfish frying—the result of my tentmate's foray into the stream by which we had camped. The two he had caught were channel catfish, the kind most often caught in the swampland bayous; they survive even where the level of dissolved oxygen is too low for largemouth bass or bluegills. Their cat's whiskers, which somehow manage to look both fragile and lethal (and are neither), are odor receptors that can scent a meal of minnows or crawfish as far as 50 to 60 yards away. These receptors, properly called barbels, help to keep the species so well fed that channel catfish often reach a weight of 15 to 20 pounds. Jim's were smallish—only about two pounds apiece—but delicious;

there is no breakfast like a hot fried slice of fresh catfish between two pieces of French bread to fortify you for the exertion of slogging through swampland.

The watery webs of intermeshing bayous increase in complexity the farther south you go in this part of the state, so that choosing a place for crawfishing becomes pretty much a matter of whim. There are some criteria, however. You want water that is neither too deep nor too shallow; a depth of two to two and a half feet is just about perfect because it provides the right environment for the tender green plants, rich in carotene, that crawfish need to grow and to produce flavorful, bright yellow fat. It is not hard to find swampy areas of that description and, after surveying a few locations, we chose one near a narrow, overgrown road that looked as if it had not been used for at least a year.

Now we had to set our nets. Each of us had brought six, mine topped by strips of blue ribbon, Jim's by strips of red, to differentiate between them—in the bayou country every man tends to take pride in his own special knack for crawfishing. It took a while to carry the nets out into the water and submerge them, baited with fresh melts (Louisianans' term for pieces of raw beef spleen). Though we both wore boots, the going was tough because we kept stumbling over tangles of long alligator weeds intertwined with water primroses. Still, these obstacles meant that there probably were plenty of crawfish around.

Such plants provide a protective umbrella beneath which the crustaceans can hide from predators like grackles and herons, raccoons and minks. Foliage also camouflages the burrow that the female crawfish digs close to the stream after the mating season in May and June, when the male deposits his sperm in a pouch on her abdomen. However, the female does not lay her eggs—or release the sperm to fertilize them—until September.

All during the waiting period, and for several additional weeks before the eggs hatch, she lives in or beside her burrow. When the eggs open, the plant cover is still of some value as a shield from birds and animals, though it can't protect the infants—perfect miniatures of their parents—from catfish, sunfish, largemouth bass and bullfrogs, which hunt them. One small sunfish, for instance, can consume about 16 newborn crawfish in a period of 24 hours. Sheer numbers usually guarantee the survival of the crawfish, certainly of the red swamp species, since a female produces an average of 400 young each season.

Jim and I dropped our nets carefully, spacing them so that no one net lay within a 10-yard radius of another, and then squatted awhile on a

A four-inch red swamp crawfish emerges from its watery burrow in the muck. It digs its refuge anywhere from 24 to 40 inches deep, plugging the entrance with a cylindrical deposit of mud. When the crawfish surfaces, this "chimney" serves as an exit.

mud embankment. The day was warming, the air now bright and heavy with spring. Across the water where the land was drier, white-topped daisy fleabane and black-eyed Susans glowed like motes of sunlight. There was a gentle hum of life around us. For a while we watched a six-inch-long spotted salamander, its shiny black body highlighted with yellow-orange blotches, moving across the back of a turtle like a small costumed lizard on its way to a fancy-dress ball. The turtle itself was of the species known as the southern painted turtle. Compared to the map turtles I had seen at Bayou Dorcheat, it was gaudy, with a reddish-yellow network across its ebony-green back and a broad red stripe from head to tail. Its highly polished shell shone like wax.

When we went back and lifted the first of our nets, it held 15 to 20 crawfish—a large catch for one lifting. They were dark bronze in color and from three to seven inches long, and they surged together as the water drained away, snapping their claws together like diminutive lobsters. We emptied them into a gunny sack and set it in shallow water to keep the crawfish moist and alive. Then we dropped the net again and waded over to the next.

The rest of the day was a continuous round of lifting and dropping, wading and sweating. When the sun turned orange over the tops of the trees the crickets began to sing in the reeds, announcing the evening. Then a low buzz heralded the mosquitoes, zooming up from the surface of the underwater forest. Mosquitoes are mostly crepuscular—active in the twilight—and so we worked hurriedly, collecting the nets and carrying the gunny sacks back to the truck. One of Jim's cousins lived on Vermilion Bayou, about an hour's drive, Jim said, from where we were. He was wrong about the distance—it took almost two hours to get there —but he was right about the kind of welcome we could expect. A middle-aged man greeted us cheerfully at the door, and his wife did not seem fazed at the prospect of boiling what we estimated to be 50 pounds of crawfish—more than enough for the four of us to eat hot, with leftovers to take home the next day.

As we sat eating by the water's edge, the bayou air rose like heat waves in the dark. Jim threw one of the empty crawfish shells into the stream. There was a loud crack as a fish snapped at the shell: the underwater wilderness of the bayous is awake both night and day. What we were hearing was a sample of the workings of a nocturnal food chain; there are as many links in it as in its daylight counterpart. Catfish are night feeders, and so are salamanders, frogs and snakes. In one of the nocturnal food chains the big water snakes prey on small blue-gills, which feed on large May-fly nymphs, which eat tiny mosquito lar-vae, which eat the infinitesimal one-celled animals called protozoa, which in turn make a meal of aquatic plants.

Early the next morning, before Jim and I set out for home, I walked to the edge of the bayou. A thick mist hung like weightless gauze above the surface of the water. Pecan trees and water oaks glinted with dew. Near the stream a hackberry lay fallen, its taproot broken in the last hur-ricane, its trunk crumbling into the earth. The bayou was thick with mud. A fish swirled to the surface—a largemouth bass, its distinctive two-piece dorsal fin an inch or more high. Apparently there were no minnows near the surface for it to chase; with a switch of its powerful tail, it disappeared underwater. A light layer of green fungus covered the back of some of the trees along the bank; the morning sunlight turned it a pale emerald color. The crawfishing trip had been more than an adventure in good eating.

The following year I went back again to the underwater forests of south-ern Louisiana. This time I brought no nets; I simply wanted to observe more of the life that lay hidden beneath the surface of the water. All of the bayous, rivers, lakes, swamps, marshes, though interdependent, are small separate worlds teeming with life. For fishermen, of course, the at-tractions are many. The oak-shaded streams and the inland lakes, lined with cypress and clogged with hyacinths, hold channel catfish, bluegill and sac-a-lait ("bag of milk," the local term for white crappie, named for its fine-textured meat). Inshore coastal waters provide speckled trout, redfish, flounder, sheepshead and black drum. Pompano, red snap-per, Spanish mackerel and king mackerel in abundance lie not far out in the Gulf of Mexico.

But it was not only fish I expected to see. I wanted a glimpse of some of the other denizens of the underwater forest: crabs, oysters, shrimp —possibly alligators. I hoped also to spot some of the fur-bearing marsh animals that rely in part on underwater bounty. An hour or so from New Orleans I veered south and east until I came to one of the marsh lakes that stud the coastal parishes of the state. In such lakes the water is brackish—a mixture of fresh water coming down from the north and salt water from the Gulf brought in by the tides. By definition, water that contains less than .10 per cent salt—one part salt per thousand parts water—is fresh; brackish water may contain from one to 25 parts of salt; marine or sea water holds at least 25 parts salt, 35 parts at full strength. The farther south you go in the marshes, the more brackish the waters generally are, but rains and floods often reverse the trend momentarily so that a fisherman can catch fresh-water sunfish one day and on another day, in the same area, salt-water redfish.

Like dissolved oxygen, dissolved salt helps determine the types of plants and animals that can live in any given part of the bayou country. Water hyacinth and sac-a-lait must have fresh water; sargasso weed and red snapper must have salt water. When aquatic plants or animals adapted only to fresh-water habitats are inundated by salt water they lose liquid, dehydrate and die. Marine plants and animals, on the other hand, accumulate too much liquid if flooded by fresh water; eventually their cells burst like overinflated balloons. The populations of brackish water remain high because there are also plants and animals, such as cattails and catfish, that can exist in either fresh or faintly brackish environments, and there are others, such as oyster grass and oysters, that thrive in both highly brackish and marine environments.

In the swamp areas through which the first part of my drive took me, there were enough patches of dry land here and there for trees to get a foothold; but farther south the earth became unrelievedly flat. This was marshland that was only a few inches above sea level; it is inundated with water so much of the year that only aquatic grasses and reeds will grow. The Acadians in this part of the state—descendants of the exiled French-Canadians memorialized in Henry Wadsworth Longfellow's *Evangeline*—have their own name for this marshland. They call it *la prairie tremblante*—the trembling prairie.

The contrast between the tree-dotted swamps and the treeless marshes was vivid. The differences between the fresh, the brackish and the salt marshes were more subtle, especially in the species of plants that predominated. In the fresh-water marshes there were clumps of grasslike wild millet and tubular spike rushes that looked like clusters of green pencils two feet high. As the water became more brackish, spike rushes now mingled with cattails, which held their plump cylindrical "tails" high in the air, and with sawgrass, whose three- to four-foot blades are sharp as knives. In the saltiest marshland, the spike rushes and cattails were replaced by woody tangles of black mangrove, about four feet tall, and by oyster grass sporting seed heads that looked like lengths of braided rope.

The marsh lake where I decided to stop had a glassy surface that reflected a sky of silvery high-running clouds. The sunlight was strong and the air hot, but even so there was a gentleness, a kind of peace and privacy, that enveloped the whole broad marshland. I hitched a boat ride with some fishermen who were trawling the lake, using two long funnel-shaped nets. After an hour or so of slow cruising we pulled up one of the trawls and examined its contents. A few translucent gray shrimp wriggled around among flipping multicolored fish. The shrimp were too small—less than half an inch long—for me even to guess if they were the common brown or white species or the rarer pink shrimp. Actually, eggs are laid several miles offshore and the newly hatched shrimp are brought into the marshes by Gulf currents; after about three months inland, when they have grown to about four inches long, they swim back to the sea to spend the rest of their lives. But spending their infancy in brackish marsh ponds and lakes is crucial; while the salinity may be low, the water is shallow and brightly lighted enough to supply the algae, diatoms and bacteria on which the baby shrimp feed.

There was also a fair collection of the blue crabs in the catch and I reached down to pick one up for closer inspection. Suddenly something else rose against my hand, and a set of razor-sharp teeth grazed the tip of one finger, drawing blood. The long, bony alligator garfish that had cut me lay quietly beside the crab, its thin pointed jaws lined with teeth sharp enough to rip a large bass in two. The gar is a strange creature; it looks like the head of an alligator connected to the body of a fish, and grows to an average length of six feet, but with a width of only about 12 inches. It is uniquely adapted for survival. Not only are its eggs toxic and thus safe from predators, but the fish itself can tolerate high levels of brackishness along with low levels of aeration because it has evolved with a special sac for utilizing oxygen more economically than most fish do. My antagonist in the trawl was still young, about 18 inches long, but already aggressive.

Returning my attention to the blue crab I had tried to reach, I saw that it was being pinched by another crab that had already nipped off one claw. The first crab appeared to have no protection at all; it lay perfectly still, not even trying to fight back. It was a softshell. During the two or three years of its life, a crab sheds its hard casing 20 times or more in the process of growing to its full size of six to nine inches across; each time it sheds its shell it is temporarily soft. During its first months, a blue crab molts as often as once a week; when bigger, it sheds every month or two, the pace slowing as it matures. Before each molt, the crab forms a soft covering that envelops its entire body underneath its hard shell; when the time comes to shuck off its old armor

*Deemed disloyal to the British Crown, Acadians*

expelled from Canada in 1775—as seen in a romanticized drawing of a century later—found eventual haven in the bayou country.

the crab can split the seams down the sides and across the bottom rim of the shell and back out in a few minutes. Then it swells up to as much as twice its former size, and within 24 hours its wrinkled soft covering smooths and hardens. Only during these hours is it a softshell. If caught earlier, during the two-week premolting stage, the crab is a buster, so called locally to describe the bursting of the old shell after the new shell has hardened. Fishermen can find a market for the crabs in any stage, but the softshells are the rarest, since they live in that state for only 24 hours at a time, and also the most prized because nearly the entire crab is edible.

Later that afternoon, walking along the lake to a place where a series of floats bobbed on the surface of the water, I found bunches of reeds that had been torn up, tied together and dropped into the water not far from shore—left by some fisherman hoping to tempt busters to hide in them. Indeed, when I pulled up a bunch, I uncovered half a dozen of the molting crabs. The reed-lined edges of marsh lakes are favorite hiding places for the crabs while they change their outer frames. And a buster needs a hiding place, for it is immobile during the final molting stage and in the softshell stage is totally vulnerable to predators, including its own kind—as I had observed in the boat. Losing a claw does not present a serious problem to a softshell because it can regenerate its limbs; but the attacking hardshell crab is a cannibal that will kill as well as maim, and the buster's only safety is in seclusion. That in turn makes it susceptible to being caught by its human predators, who inspect their floated reed bunches regularly just as a trapper runs his trap lines.

Before evening one of the fishermen took me a few miles farther south in his boat. Nameless, countless bayous interlaced as the water increasingly began to take the place of the land. Before dark we reached another lake, salty enough to have the smell of the sea. Here the fisherman thrust a pair of long-handled tongs into the water and groped around the muddy bottom with them. A few minutes later, in the late light of sunset, we were feasting on oysters that were neither too salty in their taste nor too sweet but a mixture of the two—like the waters they had grown in.

The oyster is a mollusk of interesting ways and habits. It is at the same time both well protected from the vagaries of its environment and yet helpless. In the first stages of life it is soft bodied and free swimming. Then it grows a pair of tiny shells. At this stage each oyster spat, or spawn, must find something clean and hard to anchor onto; otherwise it will sink and be buried in mud. Once attached, it cannot detach itself; it no longer has any means of locomotion. This poses a seemingly insuperable problem in terms of reproduction and continuance of its kind. How, for instance, do a male and female oyster come together? The answer is that they don't. Each sends a milky-looking substance into the surrounding water, one containing eggs and the other sperm. The sperm swim to the eggs, and they join outside the parent bodies. It has been estimated that each female sends out 60 million eggs, each male a billion sperm—adequate insurance of survival in wind-churned, muddy water. Still the problem is not entirely solved, for oysters attach themselves at random. What happens if a random group in a given oyster bed is composed of only male members of the species? The oyster has adapted itself to that possibility too. Though most oysters begin life as males, some of these become female, usually just before or during the spawning season. How oysters change their sex is a matter that scientists are still trying to explain.

Not all the creatures of the underwater forest are so docile, as I discovered on a subsequent journey to marshes still farther south, almost to the southeasternmost tip of the state, where the Mississippi Delta meets the Gulf. One spring morning I got on a small freighter at New Orleans and stayed on it as far as it went down the Mississippi to a small settlement called Venice—an apt name, since the place lies six feet below sea level. As I stepped off onto the levee there, I faced a vast grassy plain, with bayous and small lakes glinting everywhere in the distance—a reminder that almost any place at the southern tip of the delta can be reached by water, if a man has just the right kind of boat and knows how to use it.

About half a mile west of the main levee there was another embankment—a back levee built for protection from the waters of the marsh and the Gulf beyond. Between the two slopes lay a scattering of houses, and here and there purple iris and thick leaves of banana plants gleamed in the sun.

By prearrangement, I spent that afternoon with an Acadian couple, Ulysses and Odette, in their simple and immaculately clean house overhanging the marsh on the far slope of the back levee. The house, built on pilings, effectively straddled the land and the water. On one side, a door led to the levee. On the other side, a door opened onto wooden steps leading down to a boat.

The Acadians—or Cajuns, as they are usually known in Louisiana

—are people well versed in the meaning of survival. They inherited the ability to keep going from their forefathers, who were driven out of Nova Scotia (then called Acadie) by the British in 1755. After much wandering, some of the exiles settled in Louisiana, and here their descendants have stayed, despite hurricanes, floods, plagues of yellow fever and other threats that would have buried a lesser people. They are as much a part of the bayou country now as any living thing to be found in it. The house looked as if it could blow away in the first heavy wind from the Gulf. But its two strong, smiling inhabitants seemed sure of themselves. The Acadians exude a sense of safety in an unsafe world. They know the wild realm of delta and marshland, inlet and bayou better than anyone around, and are better equipped to cope with its subtle moods and sometimes violent vagaries.

The next morning Ulysses took me to see the place where the river meets the sea. We went in a small motorboat, moving downstream into a breeze that carried with it the smell of salt. Gulls swarmed in the air ahead of us and dipped low over the grasses encroaching on either side of the river. The main trunk of the Mississippi had ended, and its many roots, or distributary streams, had begun. The water was thick and muddy. Then, almost without warning, we could see the open sea. Ahead of us the brown river current met the blue Gulf and the surface was churned into foam both by the confluence of the two and by the frenzied activity of the aquatic animals attracted to the agitated water. The surface was alive with shrimp and with the thrashing tails of long, thin eels that flicked like nerves torn loose. Overhead there were sea birds—ring-billed gulls, terns and black skimmers—in incredible numbers. I had heard about the birds that streaked, circled and plunged here to feed, but I had no idea there would be so many. Their cries mingled with the sound of the waves, drowning out everything else. Finally Ulysses shouted, "Now we go back, and my brother, he show you a place tonight; a different place."

On the way back we passed a huge, irregular mound of mud in the middle of the water. This was a mud lump, a curious kind of transitory island reportedly unique to the delta of the Mississippi. When the river deposits its burden of sediment in the Gulf, it drops the heavy sand particles first; the lightweight clay particles travel farther and are the last to fall. The sand creates natural levees that extend the delta seaward until at some later stage the sand deposits begin to pile on top of the clay deposits. The weight of the sand pushes the clay beneath it downward, forcing nearby areas of clay to bulge upward. These upwellings vary from tiny underwater domes to veritable islands, some of them 30 acres in area, that rise 10 to 12 feet above the water line. Mud lumps sometimes appear suddenly, and there are tales told about ships that have been stranded on such instant islands. The disappearance of the islands is a slower process, but inevitable as the waves of the Gulf gradually wear away at the mud.

That evening I went out in another boat with Ulysses' brother Octave, a trapper. For many years Acadians who dwell in the marshes have made a living by trapping muskrats and, in lesser numbers, wild minks. In the 1930s a few South American coypu, or nutria, were imported to Avery Island, a few miles inland from the Gulf, for breeding experiments. The experiments hadn't progressed very far when a hurricane blew the door of the cage open and the nutria escaped; within a few years they had bred so rapidly in the marshes that today Acadian trappers have more of these skins to trade than the muskrat skins that once provided their main livelihood.

The nutria and the muskrat, which are aquatic animals, share the marshes with the mink. Though the mink can live on dry land as well, it is an accomplished swimmer and diver. It is also, in the considered opinion of zoologists, one of the most vicious mammals extant—"murderous" and "bloodthirsty" being but two of the ways they characterize it. The description is somehow hard to reconcile with the creature's silky dark-brown fur and its small, slender body. The male, the larger of the sexes, seldom weighs more than four pounds. But there can be no doubt of the mink's savagery when it is on the hunt for food. It will sink its powerful canine teeth into just about anything that will satisfy its carnivorous appetite—birds, fish, frogs, mice. The muskrat, its cohabitor in the Louisiana marshes, is evidently a favored morsel. Endowed with a keen sense of smell, the mink will sniff a muskrat deep within the lodge it has built as a shelter, then will claw and dig with its sharp toes until it can work its body inside the lodge entrance and seize its prey.

Fortunately for the muskrats, and for the nutria as well, their tastes in food do not generally conflict with those of the mink, although the muskrat is known to eat its own kind at times. More often it feeds on favorite vegetables like bulrushes, cattails and pond lilies, supplementing them with mussels, salamanders and other aquatic creatures. The nutria is a total vegetarian, ravaging plants from leaves to roots.

The richness of the marsh larder was everywhere apparent as Octave and I traveled along in his pirogue. This is the true boat of the bayou, made from a hollowed-out cypress log. Local people claim that a pirogue can ride on a heavy dew. It was easy to believe, as we slid over marsh reeds that grew in water both shallow and deep. The strength and the grace of a pirogue, in the hands of a man who knows how to maneuver it, are something to marvel at. Waterways only two feet wide can be negotiated; almost as if the boat were weightless, it can be poled across mud flats from lake to lake. A pirogue is easily tipped over by inexperienced users, but with an Acadian in charge there is no problem.

For a while we rode beside a flat bank that looked solid. Octave stuck the pole into the wet crust of matted growth next to the boat. The pole came out dark and glistening. The top layer of the matting was solid with plants; below it was water, then below that the matting became solid again with dead plants that had sunk to the bottom and compacted as they decomposed to form peat.

Using a paddle again, Octave propelled us easily through the marsh. As the light began to fade, we rode up a small stream that narrowed ahead, with high reeds on either side. When the moon rose, the reeds took on a white-green aura. The moonlight reflected from the surface and lay all about like a cold green glow in the warm dampness of the reeds. It was as if we had entered a world that was the color of all plant life—the essence of green.

Then ahead of us, somewhere not too far off, a quick scream rang out. It sounded strangely human, and I stood up in alarm so fast that the pirogue almost overturned. Octave grinned and pushed me back down with one hand. "Mink," he said. "She screams. The muskrat, or the nutria, she makes a noise, but not like that." He pointed ahead of the boat. "There's a muskrat."

To our right, deep among the reeds, an animal was swimming. From what I could see of its sleek back, it seemed to be almost a foot and a half long and looked like an enormous field mouse. The word muskrat comes from the Algonquin Indian *musquash,* meaning "it is red"; but this animal's fur, wet and moonlit, seemed a gleaming black. The creature was carrying plants in its mouth, possibly intending them for home construction. In the marshes, muskrats build their lodges above the surface on rafts of water reeds or cattails or patches of peat, though the entrance is always underwater. They build by packing heaps of reeds and other vegetation together, plugging in the gaps with bits of moss,

As a female alligator warily surfaces in a fresh-water marsh, a weeks-old baby, atop her head, scouts for food amidst the water lettuce.

clay or peat. The lodges look like small-scale rounded wigwams, two to three feet high.

We rode on past the muskrat, with only the sound of water for company, a soft monotonous lapping. Octave picked up a handful of flat shells from the bottom of the boat and threw them hard into the water a few yards upstream. For a moment nothing happened; then, abruptly, harsh bellowing came out of the night. It sounded at first as if a small volcano had erupted around us. The noise was full and blunt—and suddenly over. The roar of a bull alligator at night has a singularly chilling effect, one that is hard to convey to people who have never heard it. Octave turned on a large flashlight and pointed it in the direction of the noise. About 30 yards upstream a pair of eyes glowed red and unblinking. The light limned the rest of the animal. It looked to be at least five or six feet long.

The alligator inhabits the swamps as well as the marshes, both fresh and salt water, and it has had a long history in Louisiana; it has been the subject of folk tale and fantasy ever since men settled the southern bayou country. It is one of those animals whose appearance is so impressive that it generates its own exaggerated image. The reality used to be equally impressive. John James Audubon, reporting on his own observations of alligators in Louisiana, wrote in 1826: "Before the Red River was opened to steam navigation they could be seen along shores by the hundreds, or on immense rafts of floating or stranded timber, the smaller on the backs of the larger, all groaning and bellowing like thousands of irritated bulls about to fight. All were so oblivious of man that unless shot at or otherwise disturbed they remained motionless. Boats or canoes could pass within yards of them unnoticed."

The reality today is considerably less spectacular. The popularity of alligator bags and shoes in Paris, London and New York earlier in this century resulted in the drastic depletion of the species in Louisiana. Since 1963 the hunting of alligators has been illegal in the state, and gradually the population has increased; it now numbers about 250,000, and a restricted hunting season has been reopened on an experimental basis. Alligators are to be seen now all along the coast, as well as scattered throughout the swamps. People who live near the marshes have complained at times of finding alligators in their garages at night. More than once an alligator has made its way into a church meeting in one of the small communities that border the wilder areas. The result of such a visit, to put it mildly, has been confusion.

Alligators are members of the underwater forest community because they need water to keep their hides wet. The dens they construct for their winter hibernation from November through February are always at the water's edge. The females go deep into the marsh for hibernation, but for the males a canal will do. In both sexes body functions are reduced during hibernation, and there is no feeding whatever. But sometimes, on a bright winter day warm enough to entice alligators outside their dens, several of these great creatures can be seen sunning together on a bank.

Their young have a harder time of it. The female leaves its eggs in an airtight heaped-up nest of grass and mud, and departs, coming back only in the eighth or ninth week. Her young are born with an egg tooth that enables them to break out of the shell. But they cannot escape the muddy vegetation heaped over them without the mother's help. Once outside, they are on their own—prey to herons, fish, turtles, raccoons and snakes. Only a small percentage reaches maturity. Yet once they make it that far, the alligators are among the sturdiest of survivors and a formidable threat to all other creatures of their environment.

A second bellow broke the silence, and Octave turned the pirogue around to go back. The roaring resounded for what seemed like minutes; then the only sound to be heard was the water's gentle lapping. As I watched Octave poling the boat with an unerring sense of direction, it occurred to me that the ability to navigate by instinct is a gift that the Acadians seem to share only with those other inhabitants of the coastal marshes, the birds. I was to learn about the comings and goings of the birds in another trip to the wilderness some years later.

# Life among the Egrets

PHOTOGRAPHS BY VERNON MERRITT III

On spring evenings in the marshy southern fringes of Louisiana, the skies come alive with the measured beat of huge white wings as the great egrets come home to their nests and their hungry young. The marshes and beaches along the coast provide an ideal habitat for a great many aquatic birds, some transient, some that live there all year; but in spring the winter visitors return north, leaving the area to summer and permanent residents, notable among them the great egrets. These magnificent birds are the largest of the four species of egrets native to the United States, standing three feet tall, with a wingspan of five feet.

By mid-April the egrets have finished their courting and mating, have built their twiggy nests in bushes or on tree branches, and have laid and hatched their eggs. They then turn to the task of raising their young.

Egret pairs usually produce four chicks, and spend the next six weeks trying to satisfy the seemingly insatiable appetites of their offspring. The adults stalk the surrounding waters for small fish, frogs and crustaceans, which they store, partially digested, in their gullets and stomachs and take back to feed to the nestlings. By the end of May the parental ordeal is over and the chicks begin to fend for themselves.

Nesting time has its hazards for the egrets. Spring storms and floods can wreak havoc on a nesting colony. In addition, the egrets' natural enemies—hawks, raccoons, alligators and snapping turtles—are an ever-present danger. Alligators have been known to swat a tree or bush with their powerful tails to shake the young out of their nests.

The egrets had a worse enemy —man—during the days when the fashion in women's hats decreed that they be adorned with the luxuriant plumes, called aigrettes, that the birds sport during courtship and later lose. Plume hunters had almost wiped out the egrets in southern Louisiana by the turn of the century when a naturalist named Edward A. McIlhenny found eight of the birds in the swamp near his home on Avery Island and raised them to maturity. The next spring six of them returned to the island and established a colony, which now numbers some 20,000 egrets of various species. Here, and in other sanctuaries on the coast, the egrets survive and flourish, and each spring, as shown in the following pictures, they raise yet another generation to carry on.

*Like a ballet dancer sur les pointes, an adult egret poises elegantly on the branch of a dead cypress tree. It stands on its toes, as all birds do (what appears to be the first joint of its leg is actually the heel of its foot). From this carefully balanced stance, the egret can launch instantly into flight.*

*Gracefully braking before landing, and crying its monotone "cuk-cuk," a great egret returns to its nest to provide its ravenous young with food it has caught and partially digested. Each egret parent makes about four trips a day between the nest and its food larder in nearby marshes and ponds.*

*As yet unable to fetch their own food, three egret chicks keep an alert watch for signs of a parent winging home with their next meal. At this age, about six weeks, they leave the nest only to hop about on nearby branches, but will soon be making solo flights.*

The forthright technique employed by young egrets as mealtime nears is illustrated in this sequence of pictures. While its siblings sit by, the most aggressive chick—or perhaps the hungriest one—clamps a scissors hold on its parent's bill and agitates it vigorously to shake food into its own bill. Sometimes such aggressiveness defeats its purpose, as at far right, where the adult is so hard pressed it cannot disgorge any food. Occasionally the parent is pushed right off the nest.

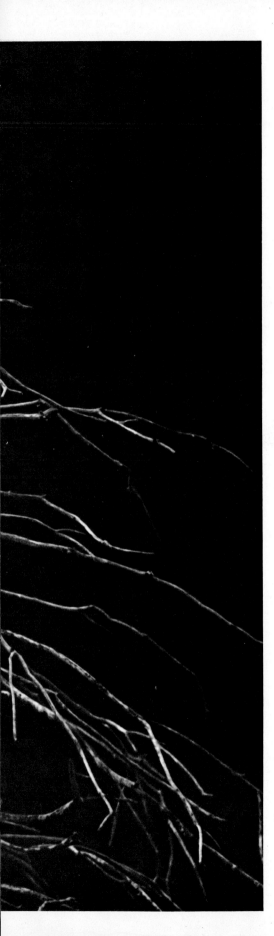

An adult egret (above) repairs the
flimsy, crudely made platform of twigs
that serves as its nest. Construction of
the nest is a shared project: the male
procures the materials, the female does
the building. Both take turns guarding
their home from twig-thieving birds.

One dead cypress tree provides sites
for two egret nests at different levels.
Some trees serve as multiple dwellings
with 10 or more nests, and suffer
the consequences: the birds' droppings,
which contain destructive uric acid,
often cause the death of a host tree.

In a no-holds-barred contest, one young
egret nips another in the neck as a
third chick watches. Often prompted
by squabbles over food, such hostility
is common during the nesting period,
and no quarter is given—though
deaths from these fierce encounters
between young birds are rare.

Having lost their down, these two-
week-old chicks look vulnerable and
scrawny as they begin to acquire their
first firm feathers. In a month they
will have enough feathers to fly, but
the spectacular aigrettes for which the
species is famous—the so-called
nuptial plumage—will not appear until
the courtship period the next spring.

With half a dozen younger birds as an interested audience, two egrets stage a noisy flap over territorial rights. Although egrets nest very close to one another, they respect certain territorial boundaries that are instinctively recognized, and that cannot be crossed except at the peril of the intruder.

# 6/ Sanctuary by the Sea

---

*Across the length of the United States . . . came the pulsing beat of far-near wings — the sound of wild geese in flight.*   McFADDEN DUFFY/ FROM BEYOND THE NORTH WIND

---

At its broadest point the state of Louisiana is no more than 270 miles wide. But its shoreline, frayed at the edge like old tapestry and fringed with thousands of islands, meanders for more than 8,000 miles. Here along the Gulf of Mexico millions of acres of coastal marsh, and the bordering beach ridges, provide one of the world's largest natural aviaries for waterfowl and wading birds, shore birds and songbirds. No fewer than 411 varieties—more than half the species known to exist in North America north of Mexico—have been sighted in Louisiana, the vast majority of them in this southern rim of the bayou country. At least 96 of these species live in and around the marshes year round.

Among the tens of thousands of permanent residents are gulls, terns, pelicans, skimmers, plovers, rails and wrens. Added to them are millions of other birds that populate the marshes part time: waterfowl from the north that arrive in autumn and stay the winter, wading birds returning from the south to spend the spring and summer breeding here, and all sorts of transients that stop by for only a day or so on their semiannual intercontinental travels.

March heralds the influx from points south, though a few species may arrive in February or even in late January. With the first warm breezes the migrating flocks begin pouring in over the Gulf. At the height of the influx, which takes place over a period of about nine weeks, more than five million of them cross the coastline every 24 hours. Many are big birds—herons and egrets and bitterns that fill the sky with flapping wings. But there are little birds too, warblers and vireos and hummingbirds. They have come from the peninsula of Yucatán across the Gulf, from the Central American isthmus or from South America. And the length of their various journeys requires a stamina that has nothing to do with the birds' size. A Louisiana heron may have flown 2,500 miles from southern Venezuela, a small purple martin 5,000 miles from southern Brazil.

Many of the incoming birds use the marshes and beach ridges merely as a stopover. The painted buntings and wood thrushes go on to other parts of Louisiana. The scarlet tanagers and rose-breasted grosbeaks travel as far as New England. About one of every 10 of the newcomers will be anhingas, ibises, their cousins the spoonbills, and members of the heron-egret-bittern family. And these will stay put along Louisiana's coastline until summer's end.

The influx from the south is spectacular enough, but it is only half of the drama. During the same months, several million birds that have wintered in the marshes—ducks, geese and coots—take wing to begin their way north along the Mississippi Flyway. This great migratory route, the most traveled of the four major American flyways, is shaped like an enormous funnel with its tip at the Louisiana coast. The neck of the funnel leads up the Mississippi River Valley, widens out at the Missouri and Ohio valleys, and continues to widen west and east until, at the funnel's mouth, the flyway almost spans the continent—from the northwestern tip of Alaska to the eastern shores of Hudson Bay.

Within this vast compass different birds take different directions. Mallards, pintails, ring-necked ducks and Canada geese use the so-called mallard route, generally northwest, to the Yukon Flats in Alaska, some 3,500 miles from bayou country. Blue geese turn northeast from the Mississippi to follow the Illinois River Valley as far as it goes. Then they continue across Canada to the Arctic tundras of Baffin Island—a 3,000-mile trip whose northern terminus is so remote even the Eskimos were unaware that Baffin was the blue goose's breeding ground until an intrepid wildlife scientist, J. Dewey Soper, tracked it down in 1929.

Although the massive seasonal movements of birds have been studied by man for centuries, the whole phenomenon of bird migrations, not only in Louisiana but worldwide, is only partially understood. Some theories about the migrations go back thousands of years. One suggested that birds flew to the moon for the off-season. Aristotle tried to account for the simultaneous arrival and exodus of species by conjecturing that one kind of bird was transmuted into another. The most popular ancient theory held that birds, like bears, hibernated, hiding in caves or tree hollows or even under the mud of swamps and marshes. Curiously, there has been recent proof that at least one species—the California poor-will—does indeed take shelter for the winter in a cavity in a canyon wall, entering a trancelike sleep and reducing its body temperature in order to survive the cold.

The poor-will is an exception, though, and a major source of puzzlement remains: why do some birds migrate while others, even members of the same species, do not? In the case of migrations southward food shortages seem to play a bigger motivating role than temperature changes. Many birds adjust to cold, even in the 40°-below of the sub-Arctic; the ruffed grouse of Labrador lives there year round. But many other species depart southward at a sign of threat to their food supply—when cold in the north, for example, begins to kill vegetation.

Just as the need for food appears to be the major southward lure in autumn, so the instinct to reproduce usually triggers the journey back in spring. The sexual glands of the birds enlarge, plumage brightens, restlessness increases and one evening the move northward gets under way. The destination of the migrant is always the same: the place where it was born, and where it will in turn produce its young.

Most migrations are leisurely affairs with daily breaks for feeding and sleeping. If the trip is to be a long one, a precautionary layer of fat will have formed under the bird's skin. In-flight speeds differ widely. Herons travel at about 20 mph, ducks and geese at 40 to 50 mph. Species with similar flying capabilities often travel together, though some flights are made up of a single species. The sexual composition of flights also varies. In the case of mallards and black ducks, the male and female fly together, courting and mating on the way north. Purple martins and red-winged blackbirds segregate the sexes in flight; the males go on ahead to establish a nesting territory before the females arrive.

Of the many questions raised by migration, the most baffling of all, perhaps, is how birds find their way across continents and seas to settle finally on the same bush or tree they occupied the previous year. Scientists have managed to pin down a few, but by no means all, parts of the puzzle. It is known, for instance, that the visual acuity of birds is two or three times that of humans, enabling them to see much more detail and to perceive tiny objects from great distances. Some day travelers seem to orient themselves by the sun; the night flyers appear to get their bearings from the constellations. But senses other than vision evidently come into play. No one has as yet satisfactorily explained, for example, the homing abilities of birds blown off course by winds, or the navigational skills invoked in cloudy weather.

Only a severe storm can force migrating birds down to the nearest available patch of ground; on the bayou coast in such circumstances, bushes may suddenly become so thick with birds that twigs and leaves seem to disappear. After one bad Gulf storm when I was a child, I remember walking along a beach on Grand Isle, a barrier island off southeastern Louisiana, and coming upon what I believed to be a bush made of birds. They were indigo buntings, hundreds of them, clustered so thickly they appeared to have grown and ripened there like berries. All along the beach other bushes were similarly laden. It was years before I learned why the birds were bunched in such incredible numbers.

Not long ago, more knowledgeable about birds and wanting to observe them in other than crisis conditions, I visited Avery Island, where large colonies of wading birds converge in spring and summer. Avery Island is a salt dome—one of 329 such curious formations along the Gulf. The domes are the product of salt beds, buried some 30,000 feet deep, formed more than 150 million years ago when ancient seas became landlocked and then evaporated. Because of the salt's light weight, it has gradually been squeezed upward by the pressure of the earth around it: most of the salt domes remain below ground level but some of them rise high enough to push the land above into a round shape. The most famous of the salt domes are the Five Islands, located inland near the shore of south-central Louisiana. Avery Island is the biggest of the five. It rises 152 feet at its highest point, and encompasses over 2,500 acres.

In 1892 the naturalist Edward Avery McIlhenny rescued eight snowy egrets from possible destruction by plume hunters and housed them in a flight-sized cage on Avery Island. From that nucleus has grown a present-day bird metropolis, a cageless sanctuary known as Bird City, complete with an artificial lake, where more than 100,000 wading birds gather during mating season. Though the site has been built up with artificial nesting platforms to supplement the trees and bushes, the birds remain as wild and free here as they are in the adjoining marshland.

The summer population begins to arrive very early in March, when budding green possesses the marshland and yellow jasmine is in bloom. As dusk descends, sharp croaking cries can be heard from afar—faint at first, then more piercing and plaintive. Flocks of snowy egrets move across the darkening sky like white arrows. They may have flown vast distances, yet when the birds first arrive at the island they show no sign of strain and they are at their most beautiful. The white of their feathers seems intensified, and indeed they are in full plumage now, for this is the start of their mating season.

There are other arrivals, too. The green heron, the yellow-crowned night heron, the least bittern and anhinga (known also as the snakebird for its habit of swimming with only its sinuous head and neck above water) cross the coastline in gleams and bursts of color, wheeling and shrieking as they descend. Little blue herons, slate colored with deep purple necks, fly in, and so do their larger cousins the Louisiana herons, their white bellies in sharp contrast to the bluish-gray feathers on their backs. From March through the middle of May the sky is filled with shafts of feathers and light, the air flooded with streams of birds, as if a rainbow had shattered and was falling in pieces into the marshes.

When they first arrive, the herons and egrets leave the sanctuary each morning for the surrounding marshes and lagoons, swamps and ponds to hunt for minnows, lizards and crawfish. But feeding is only one objective. There in the wilderness the male birds perform their courting ritual, spreading their plumes and strutting in front of the females, gurgling, taking to the air in short flights. Each male, having demonstrated both his beauty and his flying prowess, then descends to earth and to the particular female he has chosen to impress. Soon the pair seeks a branch of a tree or a bush or a platform in Bird City on which nesting will begin. Prudent instinct dictates the selection of a site; preferably it is surrounded by water on a branch at least six feet above the surface, relatively safe from tree-climbing predators like raccoons and snakes, and out of casual reach of alligators and garfish.

I watched a pair of snowy egrets that had picked the interlacing branches of a willow tree. Both male and female proceeded to flatten a place about 12 inches across, removing protuberant twigs with their bills and feet. The female then perched possessively on the site while the male went off in search of building materials. Returning with the first twig, he presented it to his mate in a great show of pomp; she raised her crest and fluffed her plumes in acknowledgment.

This is a standard ritual for the species: the male continues to procure twigs, the female to construct the nest for about three days, during which time the site is always guarded to prevent other birds from stealing the twigs for their own nests. Two or three days after the nest is completed, the bluish-green eggs begin to appear, one every other day

*Blue geese and lesser snow geese, wintering in southwest Louisiana, fly into a marshy feeding ground at the Sabine National Wildlife Refuge.*

until there are four or five in all. When brooding begins, the male and female again take turns and once the fledglings emerge both parents feed them. For the first feeding, one parent stands beside the nest and brings up some partially digested food from its gullet, nudging the newborn with its bill until they slowly respond. The young are fed several times a day, and soon they are anxiously grasping at the parent's bill the moment it returns to the nest. Between meals the young learn to walk, occasionally falling out of the tree into the water below. Sometimes they pull themselves back up, but often they are eaten by alligators.

The lessons of life in the marshland go on. One of the last—and most critical—occurs when a parent returns with a gullet full of food to a site that cannot be reached by the young unless they fly from the nest. One by one, the little birds flap over to reach the meal. After this they are ready to be guided to nearby ponds and taught to feed themselves.

With the first hint of cool weather in September and the appearance of the earliest birds from the north, the egrets, along with the other species that have spent the spring and summer on Avery Island, leave for the long flight south over the Gulf of Mexico to a warmer winter climate. Their departure is often at sunset: white wings and bodies, tinted with the deep orange of the sky, form a great long throat of light. The birds will not come back until the following spring, when they will again mate and produce another generation.

The migrations that sweep in from the north in the fall are equally memorable, especially when seen from the vantage point of one of the nine sanctuaries provided for birds and other wildlife along the coast itself. The Rockefeller Wildlife Refuge in southwestern Louisiana is one of the largest of them, 84,000 acres in extent, and last year I visited it to observe the great autumnal drama. I set out one October day just after dawn from the city of Lafayette, about 50 miles away. Cows roamed the fields along the road, followed closely by white-feathered cattle egrets looking for insects that had been stirred up in the grasses by the cattle. This species of egret is native to Africa and southern Asia, but has spread to every other continent and was first seen in Louisiana in 1955. Though generally the species is a migratory one that travels south in winter, many of the Louisiana cattle egrets inexplicably defy custom and live year round in the bayou country. Compared to other egrets, these are short-legged birds, with relatively short necks that they weave about, as geese do, when they search for food.

As I watched them, rain began to fall, heavy and violent—so thick it was hard to see ahead. I slowed the car almost to a stop and as I did so, two yellow-bellied water snakes glided across the road in front of me. In the swollen gray light, a crawfish picked its way across, claws held up. Through the rain it looked distorted, like a miniature prehistoric monster emerging from the reeds. There was another crawfish, and another—an army of them moving through the sheets of rain. A six-inch red-eared turtle was in their midst, as though being escorted to safety.

I had not traveled too far by the time the rain stopped. I was deep in marsh country. The stretches of wet green along the road were entirely flat; glints of autumn brown and yellow shimmered through the green. To the north, where the water was fresh, the trembling prairie was a sea of grass—wild millet and alligator weed. In the brackish waters toward the south the grasses were shorter but denser, their progress gulfward interrupted occasionally by low-growing black-green baccharis bushes and clumps of slender-bladed black rushes.

Water lay everywhere just below the surface, seeping through in places to form puddles and ponds. Where the water was fresh, its surface was masked by a green covering that looked like scum but was in fact made up of masses of duckweed. These minute floating plants, with leaves less than an eighth of an inch wide, reproduce so rapidly that they provide a continuous food source for waterfowl. In one pond a green-winged teal was paddling. The smallest of all duck species —about 14 inches long—it resembled a mechanical toy bobbing its head up and down as it fed on the duckweed. Then it upended itself so that all I could see was its tail as it probed underwater after some other plant. Moments later the teal was upright, eating duckweed again.

Scattered willows grew beside the road where the land had any height at all, and beyond them were russet cattails. As I neared the coast a few live oaks appeared, growing almost horizontal. The glare of the sky, a spectrum of grays, lent this seaside wilderness a look of limbo.

The Rockefeller refuge borders the Gulf for 26.5 miles. At the very southern tip of the Mississippi Flyway, it is one of the most strategically located wildlife areas in the United States and a winter home for hundreds of thousands of migratory waterfowl and marsh birds—geese, ducks, coots, gallinules and rails. The refuge has been state-owned since 1920. Under the supervision of the Louisiana Wild Life and Fisheries Commission this vast treeless expanse not only has been saved from encroaching civilization, but improved upon. To benefit the migratory waterfowl, natural ponds have been dammed to stabilize their water levels, and artificial ponds from 480 to 5,680 acres in size, called impoundments, have been constructed. Though migratory wading birds take advantage of the refuge in summer and there is a permanent population of water birds, the wintering migratory waterfowl are a particular pride of the refuge. The duck population alone, estimated at 75,000 in the 1950s, now reaches 400,000 in midwinter.

Along with the birds, thousands of alligators, otters, raccoons, muskrats, nutria and deer inhabit the refuge. The creatures are year-round residents—and so are a few research biologists. These dedicated men have a great deal to occupy them: banding birds, investigating migration patterns, pursuing the life history of the alligator and studying the entire ecology of the marsh.

As I drove in and parked near the research headquarters at the northwest corner of the refuge, a pair of Canada geese streaked overhead, their long necks stretched straight out as if reaching for some impossible destination. They were two of the 3,000 Canada geese that have been bred to be permanent residents in the refuge. I watched them circle and come down on one of the refuge impoundments. Their colors were harmonious: whitish jowls and black necks, white breasts, grayish-tan bodies and white tails. Beyond them was a flock of migrant blue geese, strutting together. In the distance, on a levee by a narrow bayou, stood a pale white-tailed deer, barely outlined against the grasses. Marsh animals tend to bleach out from constant exposure to sun and the normally rich brown coats of the deer are a reddish beige.

For a time outside the main building I talked with Ted Joanen, the chief of research. I was particularly curious to learn about the condition of the rare brown pelican. The official state bird—it appears on the state seal and hence on all state documents—the brown pelican was once a common sight on the inshore islands and the mud lumps at the mouth of the Mississippi River. In the early 1960s it disappeared from the bayou country. Scientists conjecture that pesticides contaminated the food the pelican ate and remained, harmlessly, in its fatty tissues until the pelican got into a stress situation. Then the poison surged through the bloodstream into the brain or the liver, with fatal result. Fledgling pelicans from Florida are being brought to the refuge and to a marine research laboratory at Grand Terre Island in small groups and are carefully protected. But the reestablishment of the species in Louisiana will be a slow process; the population is now estimated at only 400.

The brown pelican is immensely graceful when soaring, but an awkward waddler on the ground. It is easy to sight even from a distance,

Where southwestern Louisiana meets the Gulf of Mexico at the edge of bayou country, low tide bares a mud flat of silt, shells and clay.

because of its standing height—about two and a half feet—and its large scooplike bill. The bird is gentle if somewhat ponderous-looking, with a long neck the color of mahogany, the top of the head and sides of the neck whitish, the body grayish brown.

The pelican's quest for fish, the staple of its diet, is fun to watch. It wheels and turns in a half roll, then plunges into the sea and disappears beneath the surface. When the pelican reemerges, the pouch of its scoop bill contains several quarts of water full of fish. The bird thrusts its bill upward, contracting the pouch, and the water spills out through the corners of the mouth. Then, with an enormous gulp, the pelican swallows the fish, which it predigests and later regurgitates into the throats of its young. The babies are naked, sad and scruffy-looking. After the first soft natal down comes and goes, the birds are gray; not until the age of three do they grow mahogany-colored feathers.

While Ted Joanen and I stood talking, some of the young Canada geese in a flock nearby started a fight with another group that approached them. Within a few seconds, the gabble was such that it was almost impossible for us to hear each other. I yelled through the noise that I would like to see some of the other birds; we moved off and Joanen provided me with a guide and a station wagon. The station wagon, he explained, could go only a very short distance into the marshes of the refuge. After that, unless I wanted to use a boat, I would have to go on foot. I settled for the drive and the walk.

In this refuge, as in all wildlife refuges of the Gulf Coast and the coastal islands, the sky is never clear of birds. Somewhere overhead something is always on the wing. High above the rattling station wagon I saw a bald eagle. The great bird floated over the marsh haze, easily recognizable by its white head and white tail. Like the pelican, the eagle feeds largely on fish and is therefore rarely found far from water. And like the pelican, it faces the threat of extinction: pesticides in its diet make the bird infertile or cause its eggs to break before hatching.

Where the mud road met a stand of black rushes, my guide and I left the car and took a footpath deeper into the marsh. I stared unbelieving at the scene overhead. Green-winged teals, ring-necked ducks, mottled ducks, mallards, pintails and lesser scaup shattered the air repeatedly like fragments of an enormous explosion, as though some life force had burst apart. Though the flocks of ducks shared the sky, each kind kept to itself—a pattern they follow on land as well. Closer to the water a belted kingfisher, its crest bushy and its breast banded rust and white, hovered and waited for a minnow to come into view.

The scene on the ground was just as enthralling. Semipalmated plovers, like miniature gulls in clerical garb with single, wide gray or black breast rings under their white collars, stood curious and unafraid, watching us as we went by. A gray-brown clapper rail the size and shape of a young chicken ran across our path. Birds picked their way elegantly through the ponds, fishing as they went. The catch would be predictably good—croaker, redfish, flounder, sheepshead and other salt- and brackish-water fish inhabit the marsh waters.

Where the path ended, we came to a stop. Ahead lay reeds and grass and water: to travel farther on foot was impossible. Roseau cane and three-cornered grass rose tall around us. Then, from the northern horizon, we saw flights of migratory waterfowl heading for the marshes.

The first two flocks to pass by were American widgeons, the third shovelers. All flew in an unwavering direction, as if with the certainty of knowledge. I wondered about their numbers and whether they had been depleted along the way. Farther north along the flyway landowners have been known to flood their rice fields after harvest, forming ersatz marshes in order to entice the migrating waterfowl to descend. I am told that some of the birds are fooled and are shot by hunters. But most flocks are not deceived and continue down to the Gulf.

The flights I was watching dipped their wings over the marshes of the refuge and landed separately in different spots a mile or so from where we were standing. I could not make out the individual birds very clearly, but next day, as I was leaving the refuge, a flight of snow geese appeared on the horizon and landed in a rush only 200 yards from my car. I got out and looked at them—six adults, 12 young. The adults were a blinding white, with black wing tips; the young were a dusky gray. I looked especially at their eyes, set like those of all birds on opposite sides of the head. It occurred to me that though geese lack binocular vision, the arrangement of their eyes gives them horizon-wide vision on their journeys from Canada.

Now they began waddling about, ruffling their feathers after their flight, honking as if they recognized the place. Around them multicolored stretches of bayou country lay silent in the mist of early morning.

# The Realm of the Cheniers

PHOTOGRAPHS BY DENNIS STOCK

Along the shore of southwestern Louisiana the chenier country extends for more than 100 miles, from Vermilion Bay in the center of Louisiana's coastline to Sabine Lake in the west at the Texas boundary—a testament to the ceaseless contest between earth and water in this part of the world. It is a low-lying area with vast salt marshes, but the ridge-like cheniers relieve the flatness, punctuating the wet marshlands like elongated islands. Each long ridge, varying from two to 10 feet above sea level, represents a former coastline where waves and currents of the Gulf piled up a mixture of river sediments and broken shells.

The coast has edged gradually farther out into the Gulf, leaving the cheniers to be surrounded by marsh. The oldest ridges, now some 10 miles inland from the Gulf, were formed almost 3,000 years ago; the youngest are barely 300 years old. The more substantial of them have provided high ground where vegetation has taken root; not the lush growth of the swampy inland bayous, but a more spare, frontier vegetation. The marshes lie right in the path of the storms and hurricanes that periodically sweep in off the Gulf, and only the hardy survive; but still the chen-ier plants and creatures endure, carrying on with sturdy persistence.

Much of the chenier country is not particularly wild; men have long farmed some of the larger ridges, which extend for miles. But on many cheniers man has left undisturbed the impressive clumps of live oaks that crown their low profiles, as well as the wild flowers and small birds that adorn their grassy places.

Roving the chenier country, photographer Dennis Stock found it "a subdued, gentle and aged country, where one should not search for melodramatic proportions. There are no grand vistas here; what is provided instead is a succession of subtle experiences of discovery."

As seen on the following pages, Stock's camera recorded both vivid and muted aspects of the cheniers: the quick movement of a grackle feeding among the reeds; the splashes of brightness supplied by a species of iris known as yellow flag, by a spiny thistle and by stark white egrets; the somber colors of the hardy, moss-covered live oaks. In these trees, the classic symbols of the cheniers, Stock sensed "a strength conferred both by age and by the simple fact of having endured for so long in such a vulnerable world."

A BOAT-TAILED GRACKLE IN MARSH REEDS

LIVE OAKS AND SPANISH MOSS

*A WIND-DAMAGED LIVE OAK*

A BUTTONBUSH BESIDE A POND

GREAT EGRETS AT THE GULF'S EDGE

A YELLOW FLAG

THE FLOWER HEAD OF A SPINY THISTLE, CLOSE UP

*SUNSET ON GRAND CHENIER*

# Bibliography

*Also available in paperback.
†Available in paperback only.

Bent, Arthur Cleveland, *Life Histories of North American Marsh Birds.* Dover Publications, 1963.

Bent, Arthur Cleveland, *Life Histories of North American Wild Fowl,* 2 vols. Dover Publications, June 1962.

Brown, Clair A., *Louisiana Trees and Shrubs.* Claitor's Book Store, 1965.

Brown, Clair A., *Wildflowers of Louisiana and Adjoining States.* Louisiana State University Press, 1972.

Comeaux, Malcolm L., *Atchafalaya Swamp Life.* Louisiana State University, 1972.

Conant, Roger, *A Field Guide to the Reptiles and Amphibians of the United States and Canada East of the 100th Meridian.* Houghton Mifflin Company, 1958.

Davis, Edwin Adams, *Louisiana: The Pelican State.* Louisiana State University Press, 1959.

Drimmer, Frederick, ed., *The Animal Kingdom,* Vols. I and II. Doubleday and Company, 1954.

Dunn, Gordon E., and Banner I. Miller, *Atlantic Hurricanes,* rev. ed. Louisiana State University Press, 1964.

Hansen, Harry, ed., *Louisiana: A Guide to the State,* rev. ed. Hastings House, 1971.

*Harrar, Ellwood S. and J. George, *Guide to Southern Trees,* 2nd ed. Peter Smith, 1962.

Hochbaum, H. Albert, *The Travels and Traditions of Waterfowl.* Charles T. Branford Company, 1960.

Kane, Harnett T., *The Bayous of Louisiana.* William Morrow & Company, 1943.

Klots, Alexander B. and Elsie B., *Living Insects of the World.* Doubleday and Company, 1959.

Kniffen, Fred B., *Louisiana: Its Land and People.* Louisiana State University Press, 1968.

Kortright, Francis H., *The Ducks, Geese and Swans of North America.* Stackpole Company, 1953.

†Lincoln, Frederick C., *Migration of Birds.* United States Department of the Interior, 1950.

Linduska, Joseph P., ed., *Waterfowl Tomorrow.* United States Department of the Interior, 1964.

Lowery, George H., Jr., *Louisiana Birds.* Louisiana State University Press, 1960.

Oberholser, Harry C., *The Bird Life of Louisiana.* Louisiana Department of Conservation, 1938.

Palmer, Ralph S., ed., *Handbook of North American Birds,* Vol. 1. Yale University Press, 1962.

Peattie, Donald Culross, *A Natural History of Trees of Eastern and Central North America.* Houghton Mifflin Company, 1950.

Peterson, Roger Tory, *A Field Guide to the Birds of Texas and Adjacent States.* Houghton Mifflin Company, 1967.

Pough, Richard H., *Audubon Water Bird Guide—Water, Game and Large Land Birds.* Doubleday and Company, 1951.

Tannehill, Ivan Ray, *Hurricanes: Their Nature and History.* Princeton University Press, 1956.

# Acknowledgments

The author and editors of this book are particularly indebted to Dolores S. Dundee, Professor of Biological Sciences, Louisiana State University, New Orleans, and Harold A. Dundee, Associate Professor of Zoology, Tulane University. They also wish to thank the following persons: John J. Lynch, Biologist, Lafayette. At Louisiana State University, Baton Rouge: Harry J. Bennett, Professor of Zoology; Clair A. Brown, Emeritus Professor of Botany; Dudley D. Culley Jr., Assistant Professor of Forestry and Wildlife Management; Leslie L. Glasgow, Professor and Assistant Director, School of Forestry and Wildlife Management; George H. Lowery Jr., Museum of Natural History; William G. McIntire, Director, Coastal Studies Institute; John Newsome, Bureau of Wildlife Research. At Louisiana Tourist Development Commission, Baton Rouge: Gus Cranow and Bryce Moreland. At Louisiana Wild Life and Fisheries Commission; in New Orleans: Hurley L. Campbell; Frank Davis; Robert N. Dennie; McFadden Duffy; Allan Ensminger; in Baton Rouge: Joe L. Herring and Robert E. Murry Sr.; in Opelousas: Kenneth E. Lantz; at Rockefeller Refuge, Grand Chenier: Ted Joanen. At Lacassine National Wildlife Refuge, Lake Arthur: James Roberts, Manager, and Gary N. Burke. And also, in New Orleans: Edward Berns, Marcelle Bienvenu, Angelo Chetta, Greg T. Faulkner; A. Bradley McPherson, Assistant Professor of Biology, Centenary College of Louisiana, Shreveport; Robert E. Potts, M.D., and Mrs. Potts, Convent; Edward McIlhenny Simmons, Avery Island; John Walther, Manager, Sabine National Wildlife Refuge, Sulpher; Joe D. White, Manager, Delta National Wildlife Refuge, Venice. In New York City: The National Audubon Society; Sidney S. Horenstein, Department of Invertebrate Paleontology, The American Museum of Natural History; Geraldine Krug; Larry G. Pardue, New York Botanical Garden; and at the New York Zoological Society: Donald Bruning, Associate Curator of Birds, and Joseph Davis, Scientific Assistant to the Director.

# Picture Credits

*Sources for pictures in this book are shown below. Credits for pictures from left to right are separated by semicolons; from top to bottom they are separated by dashes.*

Cover—Evelyn Hofer. Front end papers 2, 3, 4, page 1—Evelyn Hofer. 2, 3 —Thase Daniel. 4, 5—Vernon Merritt III. 6, 7—Evelyn Hofer. 8, 9—John Launois from Black Star. 10, 11—Vernon Merritt III. 12, 13—James H. Carmichael Jr. 18, 19—Maps produced by Hunting Surveys Limited. 24—Drawings by Stephen Negrycz. 29—Thase Daniel. 33 through 39—Russell Munson. 40—Dan Guravich. 41—Russell Munson. 42, 43 —Dan Guravich. 49—Russell Munson. 50—Thase Daniel. 53—Thase Daniel; Beecher Berry except bottom Dan McCoy. 58 through 67—Robert Walch. 70 —Thase Daniel. 72, 73—Evelyn Hofer. 78—Russell Munson. 85—Thase Daniel. 86, 87—Dan McCoy. 88—Evelyn Hofer. 89—Dan McCoy except bottom left Evelyn Hofer. 90 through 93—Dan McCoy. 94, 95—Left Dr. Robert H. Potts Jr.; Thase Daniel—Thase Daniel; Dan McCoy; right Dan McCoy. 96—Dan McCoy. 97—Ann Moreton—Evelyn Hofer. 98, 99—Dan McCoy. 100, 101—James H. Carmichael Jr. 104—Stephanie Dinkins (© 1971). 107—Jan Bolte. 110—Thase Daniel. 112, 113—James H. Carmichael Jr. 117—Dan McCoy. 118 through 123 —Vernon Merritt III. 124 through 127 —Dan McCoy. 130—Thase Daniel. 134, 135—The Bettmann Archive. 140, 141 —Dr. E. R. Degginger. 145 through 161 —Vernon Merritt III. 164, 165—Dan McCoy. 169 through 179—Dennis Stock from Magnum.

# Index

*Numerals in italics indicate a photograph or drawing of the subject mentioned.*

Printed in U.S.A.